Healing the Eight Stages of Life

Matthew Linn, S.J.
Sheila Fabricant
Dennis Linn, S.J.

Healing the
Eight Stages of Life

Paulist Press
New York/Mahwah

Photo Credits
Cover: David S. Strickler; p. 2 Robert Maust; p. 24 John Glaser; p. 54 Vivienne della Grotta; p. 76 Ron Meyer; p. 98 Kay Freeman; p. 118 Gene Plaisted; p. 146 Rick Smolan; p. 178 David S. Strickler

IMPRIMI POTEST:
Patrick J. Burns, S.J.
Provincial, Wisconsin Province
September 28, 1987

Library of Congress Cataloging-in-Publication Data

Linn, Matthew.
    Healing the eight stages of life.

    1. Pastoral counseling.   2. Peer counseling in the
church.   3. Life cycle, Human—Religious aspects—
Christianity.   I. Fabricant, Sheila.   II. Linn, Dennis.
III. Title.
BV4012.2.L56   1988   248.4'82   87-35974
ISBN 0-8091-2980-9 (pbk.)

Published by Paulist Press
977 Macarthur Boulevard
Mahwah, N.J. 07430

Printed and bound in the United States of America

Contents

Dedication

To Rosabelle Fabricant
who holds us in her heart in the next life
and to all our friends in this life
who share their hearts and homes with us as we travel

Acknowledgements for Opening Stories

Introduction
Partially quoted in Harold Kushner, *When All You've Ever Wanted Isn't Enough* (New York: Summit Books, 1986), 145.

Chapter 1
Robert Coles, "Touching and Being Touched," *The Dial* (December, 1980), 26–27.

Chapter 2
Unknown

Chapter 3
Toby Rice Drews, *Getting Them Sober II* (So. Plainfield, NJ: Bridge, 1983), vii.

Chapter 4
Garrison Keillor, "Leaving Home," *The Atlantic,* 260:3 (September, 1987), 48.

Chapter 5
Anthony DeMello, *The Song of the Bird* (Garden City, NY: Image, 1982), 96.

Chapter 6
Don McNeill, Douglas A. Morrison & Henri J.M. Nouwen, *Compassion* (Garden City, NY: Doubleday, 1982), 79–80.

Chapter 7
Belden C. Lane, "Rabbinical Stories," *Christian Century* (December 16, 1981).

Chapter 8
Found at the Ravensbruck death camp.

Preface

Sometimes when I'm in the grocery store, I hear a mother loudly scolding her child who wants candy. I usually think to myself, "I hope your child doesn't grow up to be like you!" One time when I witnessed a scene like this, the grandmother appeared and began scolding the mother in the same loud voice with which the mother had been scolding the child. So often we find ourselves repeating the same behavior used by our parents and grandparents. Not only unloving habits such as loud scolding get repeated, but also more seriously destructive behaviors such as sexual abuse. For example, the Connecticut Department of Corrections found that 81% of violent sexual offenders had been sexually abused as children, often within the family.[1] Four years ago we prayed with Linda, who had been sexually abused in childhood by a relative and who later abused small children herself. After Linda forgave her relative and received Jesus' love into the hurts she had experienced as a child, she no longer experienced the temptation to abuse small children.

This book (which can also be used as a course—see Appendix C) presents what we have learned from Linda and others about healing prayer and from psychologist Erik Erikson about human development. We have used the work of Erik Erikson because he, like us, believes, "there is little that cannot be remedied later, there is much that can be prevented from happening at all."[2]

1

Introduction

If I Had My Life to Live Over

If I had my life to live over, I'd try to make more mistakes next time. I would relax . . . I would be sillier than I have been this trip. I know of very few things I would take seriously . . . I would be less hygienic. I would take more chances. I would climb more mountains, swim more rivers and watch more sunsets. I would eat more ice cream and fewer beans. I would have more actual problems and fewer imaginary ones.

You see, I am one of those people who live seriously and sanely, hour after hour, day after day. Oh, I have had my moments, and if I had it to do over again, I'd have more of them. In fact, I'd have nothing else. Just moments, one after another, instead of living so many years ahead of each day. I have been one of those people who never go anywhere without a thermometer, a hot water bottle, a gargle, a raincoat, and a parachute. If I had it to do over again, I would travel lighter . . . I would start barefoot earlier in the spring and stay that way later into the fall. I would ride more merry-go-rounds. I'd pick more daisies.

[From an interview with an eighty-five-year-old woman from the hill country of Kentucky.]

When the three of us go to the grocery store together, Matt and I head for the bacon and Sheila stocks up on whole chickens . . . including livers. The crisis comes if we get to the checkout counter and don't have enough money. For Matt and me, raised in an Irish Catholic home, bacon was a special treat served on Sunday mornings. For Sheila, raised in a Jewish home, bacon was a prohibited food not even allowed inside the house. Sheila's beloved Jewish grandmother specialized in chopped chicken liver, while the only memories Matt and I have of chicken livers are when our parents asked us to finish the leftovers from numerous chicken dinners.

Not only do we pick up likes and dislikes concerning food from our parents and grandparents, but we also pick up many other patterns. For example, statistics indicate that two out of three children with one alcoholic parent marry alcoholics and/or become an alcoholic themselves. If a child has two alcoholic parents, there is nearly a 100% chance the child will repeat the parents' alcoholic patterns.[1] Whether it be alcoholism or some other family pattern, probably the most obvious way we see these patterns repeating themselves is in the choice of a marital companion and in the choices that will follow in that marriage. Last month a friend of mine told me that her daughter was going to get married. When I asked her what the bridegroom to be was like, she responded, "My daughter is marrying someone just like her dad—just like the man I married." Because we are likely to repeat the choices of our parents not only in the choice of our marital companion, but in so many other choices in a marriage, psychologist

Hugh Missildine suggests that in every marriage there are six people: the couple and both sets of parents.[2]

Bill, a successful marriage counselor, shared with us how he focuses on the six people in every marriage. When Bill counsels, he will let whoever wishes begin by listing all the complaints about his or her spouse. Thus the wife might begin by complaining about how her husband reads the newspaper at the breakfast table or how at the supper table he doesn't even ask her about her day. Then, Bill will ask her, "How does all that make you feel?" And if the wife says, "Lonely and rejected," or "Angry and taken for granted," Bill will ask, "When did you most feel that way?" So often the wife will go back to a time in her family, as when her salesman father would leave for his trip Monday morning and not return until late Friday night. Bill finds that as the wife begins to work through the hurt with her salesman father, frequently her husband's early morning newspaper or his other seemingly annoying behavior will either bother her much less or cease to bother her at all. So often our hurts go way back to our parents, and it's not really a question of whether or not our spouse reads a newspaper in the morning. Many married persons are not bothered when their spouse does that. By healing past childhood hurts, especially those received from our family and parents, we can heal excessive reactions in a marriage or in other present situations. One of the founders of family therapy, Murray Bowen, found that if his psychiatric residents worked through past hurts from their parents, they were superior as therapists and made as much progress improving their own marriages as did other residents who were in formal therapy with their spouses.[3]

The patterns of our family and parents affect the way we relate not only to our husband or wife but to all other persons, especially to God as person.[4] I remember teaching on the Sioux Indian reservation. When I would talk about the side of God that is "Father," many of the children didn't want anything to do with that "Father" God. They feared that such a "Father" God would be like their alcoholic fathers who had erratic moods and thus would either make unreasonable demands or ignore their family altogether. On the other hand, in the time of Jesus, when he and his Jewish people affectionately called their own fathers "Abba" (meaning "Daddy" or "Papa"), they could relate to God as Father. Perhaps the reason that people in countries like Mexico seem to have a more affectionate relationship with Jesus' mother, Mary, than with God as Father is that the Mexican mother, and not the distant "macho" Mexican father, is usually the center of affection in the Mexican home. Not only Mexican mothers but also any other close relationship can affect our prayer life. I think one reason, for instance, that I find it easy to relate to Jesus as brother is that I have such a close relationship with my brother Matt.

Healing Family Hurts

Although our families influence our relationships with God and others, they do not inexorably determine them. No hurt has to cripple us. In a recent study of 984 mental health professionals, parents' lack of love and emotional nurturing was cited as the main cause of later emotional problems. But these same therapists also noted that inadequately nurtured children are not doomed to be emotionally blocked adults.[5]

We need not be trapped by patterns of our parents, nor are we to be on guilt trips if we have not raised our children perfectly. People do not passively suffer hurts but can frequently choose whether these will wound or gift them. For example, when we worked as counselors, we found people would often come with symptoms of depression. If we asked when it began, they would point to a loss and might say, for example, "When my parents died, and ever since then I've felt so much emptiness in my life." But then when we gave retreats, we would meet people who had the same losses but turned the hurt into a time of growth. For example, we met foster parents who had not only taken in an autistic child, but also during their marriage had taken in fifteen hundred other foster children. When I asked why they took in fifteen hundred children, they told me, "We were orphans, and we wanted to make sure no one else experienced the loneliness we went through." On the one hand, we had people coming to the psychiatric clinic really crippled by the death of their parents, and on the other hand people coming to our retreats for whom even death could be a gift—a gift which helped them to reach out and take in fifteen hundred other foster children.

Just how healing such a foster home can be for a child is exemplified by our friend Mary Tanner, in England. Over the years, the English courts sent one hundred troubled boys to Mary. She accepted these foster children because their only other option was jail. Each child was severely troubled. For example, one boy had attempted suicide each day and even had to be straight-jacketed. Through inner healing prayer for the hurts in his life beginning with his birth, he was totally healed. Of the one hundred boys touched by Mary Tanner's love and prayer, only four ever returned to the courts again.

How Hurts Are Healed

Not only do our behavior patterns reveal past hurts, but even physiological studies of the brain show that everything that has happened to us remains a part of us. In 1951 Dr. Wilder Penfield, a neurosurgeon at McGill University, found that if he stimulated a certain area of the brain during surgery, the patient would vividly recall a certain past incident as if it were being reenacted with all the feelings experienced when the incident originally took place. Dr. Penfield writes,

> The subject feels again the emotion which the situation originally produced in him, and he is aware of the same interpretations, true or false, which he himself gave to the experience in the first place. Thus, evoked recollection is not the exact photographic or phonographic reproduction of past scenes or events. It is reproduction of what the patient saw and heard, felt and understood.[6]

We carry not just past memories but the pain or love associated with those memories.

But fortunately our past is always present not only to us but also to Jesus. We can get untrapped from the negative effects of past hurts and turn those hurts into gifts for loving by bringing Jesus' love into hurtful memories. When we invite Jesus into a hurtful memory, we are not asking him to erase or help us forget the past. Rather, we are asking Jesus to "heal our memories" just as he did for the Emmaus disciples (Lk. 24:13–35). When Jesus joined the depressed disciples on the road to Emmaus, the disciples' hearts were filled with grief and disappointment from their hurtful memories of Jesus' death. As they shared the events of the previous three days, Jesus listened and lovingly responded to each of the ways they felt hurt. Eventually the disciples became so full of love that they could forgive Jesus, themselves, and all who had hurt them. The disciples traded their depressed hearts for Jesus' joyful, loving heart. When they left Jesus, their own hearts were "burning within them." In healing a memory, we share our heart with Jesus and take on his loving heart until we can see the past in a whole new way, with Jesus' vision. By the time the disciples arrived at Emmaus, the greatest tragedy of their lives had been transformed into the greatest gift for loving as they joyfully announced to those who still grieved, "The Lord has been raised!"

How Can Prayer Heal a Deep Hurt?

We saw the power of Jesus' love to transform the past when we prayed with Linda for healing of childhood experiences of sexual abuse. As a child, Linda was repeatedly abused by relatives. When she became a teenager, Linda herself abused small children. When she came to us for prayer as an adult, Linda still avoided small children because she feared she would again be tempted to abuse them. She felt anger at her relatives, guilt over her own sexual behavior, and a constant sense of inner darkness and emptiness. Although psychotherapy is usually very helpful, Linda's symptoms had not changed despite fourteen years of psychotherapy. During this time she had never even been able to cry.

As Dennis and I (Sheila) began to pray with Linda, we asked her to return in her memory to a time when she was sexually abused and then to invite Jesus into her memory. We thought Jesus' priority would be to help Linda forgive her relatives. Although Linda was able to recall a memory and invite Jesus into it, she remained stuck in being able to forgive. So, I tried to listen to how Jesus wanted to love Linda in her memory of sexual abuse. What I sensed in Jesus' heart was not first of all concern that Linda forgive, but rather outrage at what had happened to her. I sensed that Jesus was angry on Linda's behalf, as angry at the desecration of her body as he was over the desecration of God's temple (John 2:13–17). I told Linda what I sensed, and then we asked her to see Jesus driving out the people who abused her just as he drove out the money changers who desecrated the temple.

At this, Linda began to cry for the first time in fourteen years of psychotherapy. When we asked her why she was crying, she said,

> That Jesus would get so angry for me . . . that he would love me so much. He just wants to share all of me. If I am crying he will cry. If I am happy, he will be happy.

In this prayer, Jesus gave Linda what she needed most: to know she was loved in the midst of her hurt and anger, and even to know that her anger was Jesus' anger.

Once Linda knew she was loved in her hurt and anger, she began to forgive her relatives and herself. The following Christmas we received a gift from Linda, a picture of herself lovingly and protectively holding her two-year-old nephew. Since Linda let Jesus love her in the midst of her painful memory until she could forgive her relatives and forgive herself, she no longer experiences the temptation to repeat the ways she was hurt. Since Linda is no longer tempted toward sexually abusive behavior, she no longer needs to avoid small children.

Today, Linda works as a psychotherapist treating disturbed families, many of which suffer from patterns of sexual abuse. Recently Linda had a young patient who she sensed was being sexually abused, despite repeated denials by the child's family. Through Linda's persistence, the abuser (a neighbor) was caught and Linda was commended by the police department for helping them solve a case of sexual abuse which involved over 100 children. Linda is able to help victims of sexual abuse because the greatest hurt in her life has become her greatest gift for loving. And I was able to love Linda and sense how Jesus wanted to heal her because I too was sexually abused as a child. Although I reacted to sexual abuse by withdrawal rather than by acting out like Linda, I knew how Jesus wanted to heal Linda because I knew how he had healed me through prayer and loving friends.

Linda's fourteen years of psychotherapy had been very helpful in uncovering her painful memories of sexual abuse. But what healed those memories was to meet Jesus in the midst of them and discover that "he wants to share all of me." When Linda took Jesus' love into her past painful memories, she was freed to live out Jesus' loving reactions in the present.

As I continued to pray with Linda, I saw how the trauma of sexual abuse had caused her to become stuck in emotional development. Although much healing happened through Dennis' and my initial prayer with Linda, that prayer was only the beginning of an ongoing process of healing during which Linda is making up many years of missed emotional development. For example, when Linda first came to us, she always wore slacks and had short, straight hair that made her look like a tomboy. In groups of people, she often curled up silently in a corner, looking like a frightened child. When she spoke, especially about sexuality, she used the language of an eight or nine-year-old. In her appearance and in her behavior, Linda seemed stuck at age eight or nine—the very time in her life when the most severe sexual abuse began. During the months that followed, Linda let her hair grow and began wearing it in a curly, feminine style. She also began wearing skirts and softly styled blouses. Her whole appearance changed, from that of a tomboy to that of a lovely adult woman. Linda's language also changed, and she now uses adult terms when speaking of sexuality. I tried to provide the loving environment in which this growth could take place, by encouraging Linda's choices of hairstyle and clothing, and by gently modeling the use of appropriate words when speaking of sexuality.

As Linda made up for some of the development she had missed in childhood, other areas of missed development began to emerge. For example, Linda had difficulty establishing intimate relationships, the task of young adulthood. In the five years we've known Linda, she has gradually reached out in new ways to form intimate relationships with Matt, Dennis, myself and others. As Linda filled in some of the intimacy she had missed, she moved more fully into the adult task of generativity (reaching out to care for others), especially by generating life in her clients.

As we saw with Linda, God has built into us patterns of emotional development, stages which we go through in developing as a healthy, mature person. Hurts can interrupt this process and cause us to remain stuck in development. The grace of healing builds upon a natural process of growth, and the effect of prayer is ordinarily to mobilize and strengthen this process. The loving presence of Jesus, myself, and others enabled Linda to accomplish in a short time many years of missed emotional development.

Healing through Eight Stages of Human Development

We believe that the eight stages of human development described by Erik Erikson are a good way to understand not only our own natural process of maturing, but also the process Jesus went through as he matured in "wisdom, age and grace." (Luke 2:52) (For a chart of the eight stages, see page 23.) We have chosen the work of Erik Erikson because we find it the most congruent of any psychological system with our faith as Christians and with what we've learned from praying with Linda and others. We feel especially close to Erikson's work in five ways.

The first way we feel close to Erikson's work is his emphasis on what it's like to be a healthy person. Many psychologists have studied pathology, and we have learned a great deal from them. But Erikson believes that we cannot really understand human nature when we look at it in a fragmented state; only a healthy, integrated person can give us a true picture of what it means to be human. Erikson's emphasis on the healthy person allows him to focus on human possibilities, including the development of virtues, with its implication of spiritual development. He writes of virtue, "the Romans meant by it what made a man a man, and Christianity, what added spirit to men and soulfulness to women."[7] When Erikson begins with health rather than illness, he echoes our Christian belief that good is prior to evil, that human beings are created good and are meant to develop into the fullness of Christ. (Eph. 3:14–21, 4:13–16) As I have prayed with Linda and become her friend, I've learned that the single most important thing I do for her is to see the goodness and potential for health within her. As I see her in this way—something I believe I can do because Jesus has helped me to see Linda as he sees her—Linda becomes more and more the person I see.

The second way in which we feel close to Erikson's work is his belief that development missed earlier can be made up later, and that anything can be healed: "There is little that cannot be remedied later, there is much that can be prevented from happening at all."[8] Our entire belief in the power of healing prayer depends upon the truth of Erikson's statement, and we do see repeatedly that there is nothing Jesus cannot heal. With Linda, we've seen the effects of severe sexual abuse and years of missed emotional development gradually healed.

Thirdly, Erikson emphasizes psychosocial development (in which the main drive is toward mature social relationships) rather than psychosexual development (in which the main drive is toward fulfilling one's own sexual needs). Because of his psychosocial perspective, Erikson sees the whole community as part of the healing process. When Erikson began treating a patient, he would often go home to dinner with that patient so he could observe the family and better understand the patient's social environment. Erikson appreciates the value of what we call Christian community. In such community, God finds many channels beyond our own parents for loving us, such as teachers, friends, etc. In Linda's case, I've become a source of much of the motherly love she missed in childhood, and Matt and Dennis have become like brothers to her.[9]

Fourth, Erikson sees growth as a lifelong process with ever new opportunities to discover gifts for loving. He was the founder of what is now referred to as life span development, a view of human development that does not stop with childhood but sees adolescence, young adulthood, adulthood and old age as further stages of growth. For us, Erikson's vision of lifelong growth is like the Christian vision of how the Holy Spirit is always renewing us and leading us to fuller life.

The final way in which we feel close to Erikson is his sense of how the strengths and weaknesses of each stage of development are not a black or white choice, but rather finding a healthy balance between overusing or underusing a gift. For example, in the first stage of development, the infant must establish a sense of basic trust, the alternative being mistrust. But mistrust is not all bad, for the child who has no mistrust will soon be burned by the first hot stove he or she touches. Our own understanding of human weakness and sin is that sin is fundamentally the overuse or underuse of a gift. Sexual sins, for example, are the overuse or underuse of the gift of intimacy. Although we can say that the sexual abuse done to Linda and the sexual abuse she did to others was sinful, it was fundamentally the misuse of the good gift of intimacy. To get rid of sin, Linda did not need to get rid of strong sexual feelings, but rather she needed to channel them appropriately so they could be a strong gift for intimacy.

Human Development: A Mystery Beyond Psychological Stages

For all these reasons, we have chosen to base this book on the work of Erik Erikson, and to integrate his work with what we have learned from healing prayer. Like any gift, Erikson's system of eight stages of development has limitations and can be misused. The limitations we find in Erikson's work are areas in which other psychologies and spirituality have given us further insight into hurts and healing at each stage. For example, spirituality gives us insight into conversion experiences, prayer for ancestors and deliverance prayer as elements in healing. In Linda's case, healing included the conversion experience of discovering that "Jesus wants to share all of me," prayer for her ancestors, and deliverance prayer.[10] From psychology, we learn that recent research has revealed more of the genetic and biochemical bases for some emotional and social problems such as alcoholism.[11] Studies of prenatal psychology indicate that the first stage of life begins at conception rather than, as Erikson indicates, at birth. Some psychologists, especially women, are suggesting that Erikson's stages are biased in favor of male development and do not adequately reflect female development.

This male bias is evident throughout our culture, and is reflected in literary language that uses masculine pronouns to refer to "typical" human beings and to God. Such stylistic sexism reinforces real-life sexism, encouraging us to regard men as the primary paradigms of human and divine nature. But to continually speak of "he or she" and "him or her" is awkward. Therefore, sometimes in this book when referring to human beings or to God we will use the feminine gender "she." (For scriptural and doctrinal references to the feminine side of God, see pages 45–47 and 137–140.)

In addition to being sensitive to sexism and to Erikson's limitations, we want to avoid misusing Erikson's system. One misuse would be to see the eight stages as sharply defined, as if we were in only one stage at a time, exactly in order. Erikson's own understanding is that we are in all of the stages all of the time so that, for example, throughout our lives we are deepening the first stage of basic trust. The idea of stages of development during specific age periods simply means there is a critical period for each stage. Even as Linda was filling in missed development during the school age stage when the sexual abuse happened and thus much of her development became stuck, she was also reestablishing the basic trust of infancy and developing the generativity of adulthood.

Because we're in all of the stages all of the time and because our personalities and life experiences are so unique, we each go through the stages in a unique way. We may, for example, go back and heal the stages out of order. Linda not only began to fill in the stages from school age on, but she also went back to earlier stages. Linda's experience of being forced against her will to participate in sexual abuse had damaged her sense of autonomy, the task of a child two to three years old. In the autonomy stage, the child develops its will and learns to say "Yes" and "No." Linda's sense of autonomy had not been fully developed when she was two to three years old because her troubled mother was unable to help Linda learn to say "Yes" and "No." Sexual abuse during the school age had further damaged Linda's already vulnerable sense of autonomy. Thus, as an adult, Linda felt paralyzed in situations of sexuality and she was unable to say "No" to demands for inappropriate sexuality, or "Yes" to requests for appropriate sexuality with her husband. One way I have worked with Linda (at her request) is to temporarily share responsibility for her "Yes's" and "No's" in situations involving sexuality so that I guide her in knowing when to say "Yes" and when to say "No." As I provide the loving guidance appropriate for a two-year-old child, Linda's own sense of autonomy in this area is gradually emerging.

We go through the stages in a unique way partly because traumas or other events affect each person differently. Linda, for example, became stuck in development because of sexual abuse. On the other hand, Matt and Dennis speak about how they became stuck in development because of their brother John's death. Because John died when Matt was seven and Dennis was five, that event affected each of them differently. Matt was in the stage of school age, when industry is emphasized, while Dennis was still in the stage of initiative, when play is emphasized. Although neither Matt nor Dennis was hurt as badly or became stuck as deeply as Linda, they both show the effects of John's death. Matt's tendency is to work too much, and Dennis's tendency is to play too much.

The uniqueness of each person's process of development means that we can't use the stages as a measuring stick for completing life tasks. For example, Erikson suggests adolescence as an ideal time to choose an occupation, but many people do not make a final choice of occupation until their 30's and some even choose an entirely new occupation in their 40's or 50's. Or, the usual time for marriage is in the period of young adulthood, from 19 to 35. But a friend of ours who married at age 55 says, "I wasn't ready for marriage until now."

Growth comes not from getting through the stages on time or in order, but from receiving love at whatever stage we are in. If we let ourselves be loved wherever we are, as Linda let herself be loved in the midst of her hurt and anger, we will automatically grow.

Experiencing the Healing Process

Perhaps the main reason the three of us wanted to write this book was because of the healing we experienced when we made an eight-day retreat together. Each morning we began by reading a description of one of Erikson's eight stages. Then we spent the day prayerfully reflecting on our positive and negative memories of that stage. Finally, each evening, we shared our memories and then prayed with each other to heal any negative ones and to receive the gifts and strengths from the positive ones. In each of the following chapters, we will be sharing our experiences from that retreat and, even more importantly, we will use the same structure (brief description of the developmental stage, reflection on positive and negative memories and prayer for healing) so that you can experience the same process that has healed us and many others, like Linda.

Healing happens not only by healing negative memories, but also by receiving strength from our positive memories. A couple, whose marital problems several years ago brought them close to divorce, taught us about the power of positive memories. The husband, who is a therapist, told us all the differing counseling techniques they had tried with each other.

But none of those helped. The turning point in our marriage was one day when my wife came home from seeing the doctor. The doctor had told her that she probably had cancer. When my wife told me that, the first thing we did was cry together. And then my wife said, 'You've been such a good husband to me. When I die, I want you to promise me that you will marry someone else and give her all the love you gave me.' Then my wife shared all her memories of when I loved her—as when I built a greenhouse for all her plants. After that, we cried together and I told her all the memories I had of when she had loved me. Recalling those memories healed our marriage. They gave us a desire and a hope that we could love each other in many of the ways our hearts had forgotten.

Thus positive memories facilitate healing by allowing us to focus less on the problem and more on the love we have received. What empowers us to change is not will power, but love power. That married couple had used plenty of will power and had made plenty of resolutions over the years in trying to solve their marital problems. Healing happens as we receive love and then bring that love into hurts. Perhaps this is why 1 John 4:10 says, "We love for our part because God first loved us." Thus St. Ignatius tells us in his rules for discernment of spirits that when we are feeling depressed or in desolation, we should go back to positive memories of consolation and once again take in the love from those memories.

Much of scripture is an account of how troubled people receive strength from going back to positive memories. For instance, in the sixth century B.C. Deutero-Isaiah and the Judean people found themselves captive in Babylon, separated from their temple and land. To keep the Judeans from despairing, Isaiah compared their plight with that of their Jewish forefathers in Egypt seven hundred years previously. The early Jews experienced their captivity in Egypt as a time for understanding Yahweh's faithfulness and for forming the bonds of a great Jewish nation. Likewise Deutero-Isaiah challenges the Jewish captives in Babylon to look forward to establishing a deeper relationship with Yahweh and with each other (Is. 41:15; Ex. 14:21) just as had occurred with the Jewish captives in Egypt. Much later the Jews (under Roman domination) in Jesus' time would celebrate the Passover meal which for centuries had been a way of recapturing the positive memories of Yahweh's faithfulness to their forefathers while under Egyptian domination. That Passover meal with its cup of blessings, that celebration of positive memories, is what Jesus chose for the setting when he wanted to institutionalize the Eucharist. Thus it is no surprise that "Eucharist" in Greek means "to give thanks" and is an invitation to daily celebrate and allow Jesus' love to renew us especially through our positive memories.

As we become rooted in Jesus' love, he will empower us to turn our negative memories from times of hurt into times of gift just as he did in his own life. Thus Jesus turned his childhood hurt of being a refugee and stranger in Egypt into a gift to love outcasts and Samaritan strangers, or his adolescent hurt of his foster father Joseph's death into a gift of longing for "Abba" as Father, or his adult hurt of seeing all his efforts fail into a gift for compassion for those like the good thief (Lk. 23:39) who considered themselves failures. Jesus promises us that the greatest hurts in each of life's stages will become our greatest gifts. Dag Hammarskjold's motto is our prayer for this book: "For all that has been—Thanks! To all that shall be—Yes!"[12]

EIGHT STAGES OF LIFE

According to Erik Erickson
From *The Life Cycle Completed*
(New York: W.W. Norton, 1982), pages 32–33.

Stages	Psychosocial Crises	Virtue	Radius of Significant Relations
1. Infancy Until age 2	Basic Trust vs. Basic Mistrust	Hope	Maternal Person
2. Early Childhood Age 2–3	Autonomy vs. Shame & Doubt	Will	Parental Persons
3. Play Age Age 3–5	Initiative vs. Guilt	Purpose	Basic Family
4. School Age Age 6–12	Industry vs. Inferiority	Competence	Neighborhood, School
5. Adolescence Age 12–18	Identity vs. Identity Confusion	Fidelity	Peer groups and outgroups; Models of leadership
6. Young Adulthood Age 19–35	Intimacy vs. Isolation	Love	Partners in friendship, sex, competition, cooperation
7. Adulthood Age 35–65	Generativity vs. Stagnation	Care	Divided labor and shared household
8. Old Age After 65	Integrity vs. Despair	Wisdom	"Humankind," "My Kind"

Chapter 1:

Infancy (Trust vs. Mistrust)

Where Does Inner Strength Come From?

In the spring of 1961, psychiatrist Dr. Robert Coles was studying black southern children struggling to de-segregate schools against extremely discouraging odds. As Dr. Coles watched four six-year-old Louisiana black girls respond to constant harassment with quiet courage, he wondered what could give these impoverished and vulnerable children such resilience. None of his intricate social science explanations could account for it. Then he heard this from one Louisiana black mother:

"My child comes home from school, and she's heard those white people shouting, and she's not going to show them she's scared, not for a second, but she is scared. I know she is. And the first thing she does is come to me, and I hold her. Then she goes to get her snack, the Oreos and juice, and she's back, touching me. I'll be upset myself, so thank God *my* mother is still with us, because I go to her, and she'll put her hand on my arm, and I'm all settled down again, and then I can put my hand on my daughter's arm! Like our minister says, the Lord touches us all the time, if we'll just let Him, and He works through each of us, so when my mother puts her hands on me, and I put my hands on my child—it's God giving us strength."

[Robert Coles, "Touching and Being Touched"]

A recent experiment demonstrated how we learn trust. Money was left in a phone booth and found by the next caller. The experimenter approached, said the money was his, and asked if he could have it back. The money was seldom returned unless the experimenter did one thing: touch the other person. Touch formed a bond of trust because we learn trust and mistrust, according to Erikson, primarily in the first stage of infancy and especially through the ways the infant is touched and held.

The story of Old Anna illustrates what Erikson means when he says that the establishment of basic trust is the task of infancy. The story begins in 1915, when Dr. Henry Chapin, a New York pediatrician, reported on his study of children's institutions in ten U.S. cities. He found that in all but one of these institutions virtually every child under two years of age would die, regardless of the quality of medical care the children received. In stark contrast, Dr. Fritz Talbot shared his experience of visiting the Children's Clinic in Dusseldorf, Germany, where the mortality rate for children under the age of two nearly equalled that for the general population. Dr. Talbot had studied everything at the Children's Clinic that he thought was involved in good care of a child: food, sanitation, nursing care, etc. But he could not find anything substantially different from what was being done in children's institutions in the United States.

One day Dr. Talbot visited a very neat and tidy ward with the director of the Clinic, and he noticed an old woman carrying a baby on her hip. The old woman didn't look at all like a nurse. He asked the director, "Who's that?'' The director said, "That is Old Anna. When we have done everything we can medically for a baby and it is still not doing well, we turn it over to Old Anna and she is always successful." Old Anna was the only thing that made the Children's Clinic different. She was picking up the babies when they cried, holding them, and giving them motherly love. A few minutes of motherly love from Old Anna meant the difference between life and death for those babies.

When Dr. Talbot came back to the U.S., he told American doctors what he had learned in Dusseldorf about the importance of motherly love. He was contradicting the most famous pediatrician of the time, Dr. Luther Emmett Holt, Sr., who wrote *The Care and Feeding of Children*. First published in 1894 and in its fifteenth edition in 1935, his book was the "Dr. Spock" for his generation. Dr. Holt advocated regimented feedings by the clock, not picking up babies when they cried, and not "spoiling" them with too much handling. Despite Dr. Holt's popularity, some children's institutions did listen to Dr. Talbot's teaching on the importance of motherly love and they brought in women volunteers to do nothing but hold the babies. In a later study of such institutions, the mortality rate for children under the age of two had decreased to that of the general population.[1]

Old Anna illustrates what Erikson says about establishing trust in infancy. At this stage, the child lacks a separate sense of identity and depends on others to meet its needs. An infant is not totally passive, since it has many ways of making its needs known, as all parents know . . . but an infant cannot do much about meeting those needs. If an infant were to wear a t-shirt, the shirt might say, "I am what I am given." The infant's whole way of being is to take in, to receive from others. Erikson says that basic trust is established not so much through quantities of love and attention, but through the quality of love the child receives. Perhaps that is why just a few minutes of Old Anna's love could mean the difference between life and death for a baby. In those few minutes, Old Anna would give a baby everything she had, and she would give it in the way babies understand best: through touch.

In Bogota, Colombia earlier this year, we experienced what Dr. Talbot learned from Old Anna seventy years ago. We visited the San Juan de Dios Hospital where, until recently, 60% of premature babies died. Doctors had treated these babies by the traditional method of placing them in incubators. Then, Dr. Hector Martinez began the "Kangaroo Program." When a premature baby is born, no matter how tiny and unless it has a serious infection, Dr. Martinez immediately puts it inside the mother's blouse . . . and leaves it there for up to four or five months. When the mother needs a rest, the father carries the child in his shirt. The death rate for these babies who are never deprived of loving touch during the first months of life is only 5% compared to the previous death rate of 60%.[2]

Touch Builds Trust

Babies like those in the Kangaroo Program understand touch because the skin is our largest and neediest sense organ, and it is also the earliest to develop. Without touch, even physiological systems will not function properly. For example, physical handling in early life directly affects the actual growth of the brain. The more a child is touched, the heavier the brain, whereas if an infant is not touched or nursed sufficiently very early in life, this may affect later intelligence more profoundly than formalized education.[3]

Besides physical consequences, deprivation of touch also has emotional and social consequences. Studies of adolescents found a positive correlation between drug abuse and home environments having little or no touch.[4] Another study, of 49 different cultures, found that in 48 of the cases, more violence and cruelty occurred in cultures with less touch, and less violence and cruelty occurred in cultures with more touch.[5] Perhaps for this reason psychotherapist Virginia Satir says that even as adults we need four hugs a day for survival, eight for maintenance and twelve for growth![6]

The three of us take Dr. Satir's advice seriously as we rediscover the power of touch to help us grow in trust when we are having difficulty communicating. A misunderstanding or hurt feeling that might take hours to resolve by just talking about it will often be resolved in just a few minutes if one of us reaches out to touch or hug another while we speak.

How Important Is a Father's Love?

Although a mother's touch and care is critical during infancy, babies need touch and care from fathers too. But frequently fathers have difficulty interacting with an infant. The average father interacts with his infant during its first months only from two to seven times a day for an average of only 37.7 seconds.[7] When fathers have little or no opportunity to interact and bond normally with an infant, abnormal "bonding" behavior may result, such as the high amount of incestuous behavior among stepfathers who never had the chance to bond with their stepdaughters as infants.[8] Other studies of father absence report detrimental effects ranging from high delinquency rates and low intelligence scores to premarital pregnancy.[9]

But when fathers do interact with their infants, those infants thrive. Yale researchers studied seventeen infants between two and twelve months of age, whose fathers stayed home to raise them while their mothers worked. When tested against infants that stayed home with their mothers, the infants that stayed home with their fathers tested six to twelve months ahead in problem solving abilities and two to ten months ahead in social skills. These infants who stayed home with their fathers developed so quickly because, unlike many working fathers, their working mothers developed close attachments to their babies by interacting with them after work. Thus these infants grew up securely surrounded by the love of two parents rather than one. When tested again two years later, these children's rate of development had not slowed down.[10]

Trust Begins in the Womb

We believe the child is sensitive to the love of both its parents long before birth, and that the first stage of trust vs. mistrust begins at conception. Many psychotherapists agree with us that the child in the womb is sensitive to love and can be hurt by lack of love. Some psychotherapists, such as Frank Lake, R.D. Laing, David Cheek and D.S. Winnicott, even believe that most psychoses begin in the womb or as a result of birth trauma, while neuroses develop later.[11] Psychoses are the most serious form of mental illness, in which a person has completely withdrawn from reality, while neuroses are less serious.

Our belief that the first stage of life begins in the womb

is based upon current research in prenatal psychology and upon our experience with healing prayer. Before current research in prenatal psychology, medical science taught that a child could not remember before the age of two because his central nervous system was still too immature. This view began to change in 1948, when David Spelt proved that a fetus could learn a conditioned response to a loud noise and remember it for up to three weeks.[12] Today several theories explain how a fetus can remember, perhaps even from conception.[13,14] Regardless of what theory you choose as an explanation, much experiential evidence suggests that the child in the womb does remember. For example, Linda Mathison began to collect experiential evidence for early memory after her two-year-old son shared what sounded to Linda like prenatal and birth memories. After Linda asked other parents if they had similar conversations with their children, she received over 1000 accounts of what appear to be prenatal and birth memories in children under five years old.[15]

One of the most dramatic illustrations of memory in the womb is the work of psychotherapist Dr. Andrew Feldmar. He had three patients who repeatedly attempted suicide, each one on the yearly anniversary of previous attempts. The dates seemed meaningless until Dr. Feldmar realized that each of these patients was attempting suicide at a time which would be the anniversary of their second or third month in the womb. When he investigated their histories, he discovered that the dates of the suicide attempts were the dates when their mothers had attempted to abort them. Not only was the timing of each patient's suicide attempt reminiscent of an earlier abortion attempt, but even the method was similar. One patient whose mother had tried to abort him with a darning needle tried suicide with a razor blade. Another, whose mother had used chemicals, tried suicide with a drug overdose. When Dr. Feldmar's patients realized that their suicidal ideas were really memories of their mothers' attempts to kill them, they were freed from the compulsion to commit suicide.[16]

What Do Babies Remember?

Because the life of the child in the womb is so intimately connected with the life of its mother, the child's memories are connected with its mother's experiences and reactions. This relationship can be understood physiologically because every emotion we feel produces hormonal and chemical changes in our bloodstream. When a pregnant woman feels fear, anger, joy, peace, etc., the changes in her blood chemistry are shared across the placenta with her child.[17] Just how quickly mother and child can share feelings is demonstrated by an experiment in which pregnant women were told their babies weren't moving. Each woman became alarmed that something was wrong with her baby, and within seconds the baby (observed through ultrasound) was kicking . . . apparently in response to its mother's fear.[18]

Dr. D.H. Stott has done the most long-term research to date on the lasting effects of prenatal stress. He found a direct one-to-one correlation between certain kinds of stresses in the mother during pregnancy and later physical and emotional problems in the child, such as stomach disorders and hyperactivity. The stress of prolonged marital discord during pregnancy had a greater effect than physical illness, accidents or even deaths of close relatives.[19] In a study of over 1300 children and their families, Dr. Stott

found that a woman in a tension-filled marriage runs a
237% greater risk of bearing a child with physical and emotional problems than a woman in a loving relationship.[20]
An extreme example is the wife of an alcoholic wife-bat-
terer, who finally left her husband during her pregnancy,
only to have him try to force her to return and even throw
a brick through her window. Twenty hours after birth, her
child vomited fresh blood and died. An autopsy revealed
three peptic ulcers.[21]

Fortunately, babies can absorb and remember love
and enjoyment as well as stress and trauma. For example,
Boris Brott is a symphony conductor who was able to play
the cello line from certain pieces of music which he had
never seen before, as if he already knew the score. He
learned from his cellist mother that she had performed
these selections while pregnant with him.[22] Recent scientific research confirms that the fetus not only hears and re-
sponds to music, but also interacts with it and can
distinguish between various kinds of music.[23]

The love of parents is the most important thing that
children experience in the womb, and it can overcome the
negative effects of many stresses and traumas. Dr. Franz
Veldman, a Dutch scientist who developed "haptonomy,"
the science of touch, teaches parents to make loving contact with their unborn child. A mother and father can communicate with a fetus by placing their hands on both sides
of the womb. If they send their love especially through the
hands on the right side of the womb, the child will begin
to move over to the right side and curl up with its neck under those hands. If they then send their love through the
hands on the left side of the womb, the child will move to
the left side and curl up under those hands. In this way,
the parents can carry on a loving dialogue with the child.
They can do this beginning when the child is about 4¹/₂

months in the womb (or whenever it is large enough for the mother to feel movement) and until about seven months (or whenever it is too large to be able to move freely). If the parents communicate with their child in this way each day at the same time and then miss their "appointment" with the child one day, the child will begin to kick, as if protesting even this momentary loss of loving communication which it has learned to expect.[24]

Early Hurts Can Be Healed

Sometimes when we speak of how sensitive the child in the womb is to the presence or absence of love, a frightened and guilty-looking parent will approach us. Such a parent will ask if there is any hope for a child who was conceived during a stressful time in the life of the family or who experienced severe trauma at birth. Dr. Jerome Kagan emphasizes the power of a loving environment to heal prenatal and birth trauma when he says,

> If a pregnant mother is tense or ill for most of the pregnancy, the probability of a premature birth is increased. And infants born prematurely are different psychologically during the first year or two of life. But if the environment is supportive of growth, psychologists are unable to find any differences between six-year-old children born prematurely and those born at term. The experiences of the intervening six years are able to repair or change the psychological profile of the premature infant.[25]

Our experience with healing prayer confirms Dr. Kagan's optimism that hurts in the womb and at birth can be

healed. The only reason we speak of such hurts is to en-
courage people to pray for healing. Barbara Shlemon tells
the story of how a baby who was profoundly hurt in the
womb received healing. When Barbara met seven-month-
old Jennifer, she was still at her birth weight of six lbs.
Since the doctors had never seen a more retarded child,
they recommended placing Jennifer in an institution. Barbara learned from Jennifer's mother that she had suffered
three previous miscarriages and expected to lose Jennifer
also. The mother, certain that this would happen, raised all
her defenses against giving life to Jennifer so that she
would not have to go through losing her. She communicated to Jennifer, "Don't come to life because we can't handle losing you." When Jennifer was born, she was literally
unable to receive life and could not assimilate any nourish-
ment. Barbara prayed for the hurts Jennifer experienced in
the womb, asking Jesus to be with her in the womb and call
her to life by telling her how much she was loved. Within
three weeks after this prayer, Jennifer grew to the normal
weight for an eight-month-old and at age 18 months she
was learning to speak and walk.[26]

If the child does receive the love and nurturing it
needs during the stage of infancy, then it will decide—as
Jennifer ultimately decided—that the world is good and
can be trusted. Perhaps that's why a universal image of
trust in painting and sculpture is a child nursing at its
mother's breast. Not only will the child decide that it can
trust the world, but it will also decide that it can trust itself,
because it sees that its needs (and therefore its being) bring
a good response. It's as if the child says, "Something good
happens when I express my needs. My needs must be
good. *I* must be good."

Such a child will be able to move on to the next stage
of development with a foundation of basic trust. The res-

olution of each stage's task is a matter of balance rather than an all-or-nothing choice. In establishing trust, for example, the child needs some mistrust to protect it from those things which really are harmful. But the child who successfully resolves the task of the first stage will emerge on the trust side of the continuum between trust and mistrust. As the child faces the transition to the next stage, perhaps through events such as weaning from the mother or the birth of the next child, it will be able to draw upon the strength that comes from basic trust.

If the infant's needs for love and care are not met, it will mistrust and probably withdraw into itself, perhaps from all relationships. It will distrust the world and also itself, feeling that it is empty and no good. It will blame itself, because children blame themselves for everything and if a child's needs are not met it assumes those needs are bad. If there is extreme deprivation of love or sudden abandonment, the child may go into a chronic state of mourning and perhaps be depressed for the rest of its life unless healing comes later. In some cases, such as the children who were left in orphanages without someone like Old Anna, unloved babies will literally die of mourning. Medical doctors now recognize the fatal consequences of severe deprivation of love to the extent that they've given this condition a name: "marasmus."[27]

Type A Behavior—Lack of Basic Trust?

In less severe cases, the failure to establish basic trust can have physical, emotional, social and spiritual consequences for later life. For example, the well-known research of heart doctors Friedman and Rosenman on Type A behavior began when they were having their medical office chairs reupholstered. The upholsterers said that the wear pattern on the chairs looked as if the people who used them were always "sitting on the edge of their chairs." Drs. Friedman and Rosenman identified those who have the highest incidence of heart attacks as "Type A" people. Such Type A people are characterized by hostility, anger, chronic speed and impatience, in contrast to the more relaxed and easy-going Type B people, who have fewer heart attacks.[28] The research of Dr. Redford Williams and his colleagues at Duke University confirms the relationship between hostility and heart disease, and suggests that the hostility of the Type A adult is a consequence of a failure to establish basic trust in childhood.

> *Hostility* is considered to be an attitudinal set (perhaps even a personality trait) which stems from an absence of trust in the basic goodness of others and centers around the belief that others are generally mean, selfish and undependable. We feel it likely that this attitude is, to a large extent, learned from caregivers early in life. From the developmental perspective, it may reflect an incomplete development of 'basic trust,' to use Erikson's (1963) term.[29]

Dr. Williams and his colleagues suggest that the physiological link between hostility and heart disease is the excessive secretion of certain hormones related to states of vigilance, and the Type A person secretes more of these hormones because,

> . . . since he/she is unable to depend upon the good behavior of others and must, indeed, be on guard against their bad behavior, the hostile

Type A person might be expected to spend a good bit of the waking hours in a state of vigilant observation of those about him/her.[30]

Basic trust is crucial not only for physical health but also for later emotional development because without it we cannot grow by letting go of the past and risking new possibilities in the future. At each stage in life, we become attached to what is familiar within ourselves and in our environment, and only a foundation of basic trust can give us the courage to let go of what is familiar and step into the unknown. For example, homosexuality and lesbianism may often be the result of a failure to establish basic trust with the parent of the same sex. Thus insecure in his or her identification with the more familiar same-sex parent, the homosexual or lesbian is unable to step into the more unknown world of relationships with the opposite sex.[31] Not only is the person without basic trust handicapped in normal emotional development, such as the capacity for heterosexuality, but this person may find it especially difficult to recover from traumatic events such as the loss of a loved one. Such a loss is a blow to anyone's sense of basic trust, but a healthy person will be able to rely on a reserve of previous trustful experiences. A person wounded in basic trust, however, is more likely to be shattered by a death and find the grieving process much more difficult. "Thus, basic trust is a key resource that facilitates a bereaved person's ability to grieve and to grow."[32] As well as contributing to physical and emotional illness, lack of basic trust has social consequences and may be the basis for much antisocial or psychopathic criminal behavior. I (Sheila) saw this several years ago when I had just been through the most painful and destructive experience of my life. I felt betrayed by the people I had trusted most and to whom I felt most vulnerable. For a period of time, it seemed to me that all trustworthiness was gone from the universe. I was experiencing the way a severe trauma can shatter what we have accomplished in earlier stages of development.

Once during that time, I was shopping in a grocery store. When I paid the cashier, she gave me too much change. I automatically returned the extra money to her. I had always done the same thing in similar situations, but I noticed that this time something was different. Previously, I returned extra change with a sense that I was doing something intrinsically meaningful. I experienced myself as part of a fabric of relationships based upon and held together by trust, and I wanted to add to the level of trust within the human community rather than detract from it. But I realized that in this case I had returned the extra change solely out of a habit of honesty, without any sense of honesty as intrinsically meaningful. It was months before I began to regain any sense of trustworthiness in the universe. During those months, so far as I know, I continued to return extra change, tell the truth and in other ways maintain my usual level of honest behavior . . . but solely out of habit.

Reflecting later on this experience, I saw that trust underlies all moral and ethical behavior. I had established enough basic trust in early life to develop a habit of honesty. That habit was deep enough to endure during a time in my life when all trust was gone. Now, when I read newspaper accounts of psychopathic criminals, I think, "What if I had never experienced trust in infancy? Would I have any reason to behave honestly? Would I be any different from this person I'm reading about?"[33]

Spiritual Consequences: Trust and Our Image of God

Basic trust affects us spiritually as well as physically, emotionally and socially. When I (Sheila) was a student in theological school, I had an experience that taught me how deeply our image of God is related to the ways our parents treated us, and how a failure to establish basic trust in infancy can have lifelong spiritual consequences. During one period in my theological education, I was reading books by several German theologians, all born in the early part of this century. In each of these books, I sensed an image of God as remote and unapproachable, and human life seemed to be a long search to find God. Only rarely would we feel God near to us, and the rest of the time we were to bravely walk in darkness. I felt very concerned by this attitude toward God, since it had not been my own experience. I had always experienced God as warm and approachable, rather like my Jewish grandfather and grandmother. I shared my concern with one of my teachers, a woman who was married to a German scripture scholar. She said, "You know, at the time when my husband was brought up in Germany, parents did not pick up or hold their babies when they cried. The parents thought this was the best way to develop self-discipline in their children." As I heard this, I thought, "I wonder if these theologians who are crying out to a distant God are really crying out to a mother and a father who never picked them up and held them."

The way in which we see God is shaped by the ways our parents treated us, and the way in which we see God also determines who we will let God be for us and how much we can let God give to us. If our image of God is wounded, we can get into a vicious cycle in which we pray and pray for healing, but no healing comes because we're praying to a God who only reinforces our hurt. In the case of these German theologians, for example, they were desperately in need of God's intimate love to heal the mistrust and despair that come from emotional deprivation in infancy. Yet their attitude toward God led them to pray in very formal ways and I doubt they would have been comfortable crawling up on Jesus' or Mary's lap and letting themselves be loved intimately in prayer. These theologians who were shaping the whole Christian world's image of God through their books were praying—and encouraging others to pray—in ways that only reinforced a distorted image of God.

How Can Our Image of God Be Distorted?

At each stage of development, our image of God can be distorted by whatever ways we were not loved, and these distortions will be the roots of those patterns of sin to which we become most vulnerable. In the stage of infancy, mistrust and despair can affect our image of God in several ways. The German theologians, for example, seem to have seen God as a reluctant parent to whom they had to cry out long and loud before they would be heard. Such an attitude concentrates what little trust and hope there is on ourselves as able to get God's attention after long crying, and it focuses mistrust and despair onto God. The patterns of sin which are likely to emerge in later life will be based upon inability to surrender to God.

Another distortion at this stage might be to focus our mistrust and despair on ourselves, and with whatever trust and hope we have, to see God as a rescuing parent who comes down to save us from our rottenness. Such an attitude might be called "Christian Wormism," since it emphasizes what lowly, wormlike creatures we are. The patterns of sin that can emerge from this attitude are based upon a contempt for ourselves and the rest of God's creation (rather than seeing creation as fundamentally good, although flawed by original sin). Such an attitude can lead us to passively wait for God to rescue us from this rotten world rather than working together with God to redeem creation and bring it to fulfillment. God hates sin, but loves persons who become sinners and never forgets their fundamental goodness. Finally, if we have so little trust and hope that we see both ourself and God with mistrust and despair, our image of God may be of a wrathful parent, a God who punishes us miserable creatures because we deserve it. We will see suffering as deliberately sent by God, and will do nothing to avert it because it is our just punishment.

But if we have received enough love during the stage of infancy and have established basic trust, we are likely to be able to trust God and also have a foundation for the virtue of hope. Each of Erikson's stages provides the foundation for a virtue, and the virtue for this earliest stage of infancy is hope. Thus, the infant whose needs are met in such a way that it can learn to trust the world and itself will probably be able to move into a relationship with God that has mutual trust and hope at its core. God is good, and so are we as God's creatures. Scriptural images for such an attitude include God's pronouncement over creation in Genesis 1:31, "It was very good," and Wisdom's affirmation of God's love for creation, "For you love all things that exist, and have loathing for none of the things which you have made." (Wis. 11:24) Mary's Magnificat is based upon trust and hope in both herself and God, when she says, "From now on all generations will call me blessed, for the Mighty One has done great things for me, holy is his name." (Lk. 1:48–49)

Parenting not only shapes how we trust in God, but also how we trust in God shapes how we parent. Not only does Erikson speak of trust in loving parents as the basis for religious faith, but he also speaks of how parents need religious faith in order to give their children basic trust. Parents who know themselves as held in the arms of a loving God can hold their own children with a security beyond themselves. In contrast, parents who must survive in the face of an impersonal or even hostile Reality will be able to give their children only a limited sense of trust. Thus Erikson can say, "many are proud to be without religion whose children cannot afford their being without it."[34]

Prayer & Trust

The gift of prayer that can come from this stage is contemplative prayer. In contemplative prayer, we become like a child peacefully nursing at its mother's breast. We can be still and do nothing but rest and receive from a God who wishes to fill us with good things. Contemplative prayer presumes that God and goodness are found not only "out there," but also within the depths of ourselves. We are good, and when we become still and centered we will find God within. Religious groups which see human beings as basically depraved usually do not have a developed tradition of contemplative prayer since they are suspicious of what we will find when we go within. In contrast, religious groups which see human beings as basically good also have a tradition of contemplative prayer in which God can be found in the depths of our own selves.

Such traditions emphasize a God who is loving and ourselves as lovable.

Just as unloving parents can distort our image of God, so those moments when we have given or received parental love can heal our image of God. The child whose earliest experiences of crying out at night are followed by being gathered up in the arms of a loving father, or who is fed at the breast of a mother whose eyes convey, "You are uniquely precious in all the world"—such a child, whose immediate reality has been trustworthy, will become an adult who can have faith in ultimate Reality. The early Christians sensed this connection between faith and trust by using the same Greek word, *pistuo*, for "faith" in God as for "trust" in a parent.

Jesus also associated trust in a loving parent with faith in a loving God. Jesus encouraged people to call God "Abba," meaning "Daddy" or "Papa." For Jesus, the use of "Abba" was not meant to reveal God only as a *male* person (as opposed to a female person), but rather as an *intimately parental* person (as opposed to the distant, patriarchal God-image of his day).[35] Jesus also uses feminine imagery to describe God. For example, in Luke, Jesus tells three parables of the merciful forgiveness of God, and in the second one he presents God as the woman householder who searches for a lost coin (Lk. 15:8–10; see also Mt. 23:37, 13:33).[36] In speaking of God as feminine and maternal, Jesus was drawing on the Old Testament. For instance, Isaiah speaks of God as a loving mother in labor and the author of the Book of Numbers speaks of God as one who gives birth, breastfeeds, and carries the child in her bosom (Num. 11:12; see also Ex. 34:6, Dt. 32:18, Is. 49:15, 63:15, 66:13, Ps. 131:2). Male and female, loving mothers and fathers reflect for us the image of God (Gen. 1:27).

Although our human experience of persons can never exhaust the nature of God, Jesuit spiritual director Fr. Tony deMello says that if we're going to make God a person, we need to make God at least as good as the best of us. God is more father than the best human father, more mother than the best human mother. On September 10, 1978, in a public address, Pope John Paul I said,

> We are the object of a never-failing love on God's part. We know that he always has his eyes open to us, even when it seems to be night. He is a father; more than that, he is a mother. He intends to do us no harm; he wants to do only good to everyone.[37]

John Paul I speaks of God as both father and mother. The encyclical "Rich in Mercy" by his successor, John Paul II, expresses this when it speaks of the divine mercy of God as having two aspects, described by two Hebrew words. *Hesed* means God's fidelity, the fatherly love of God, in which God is faithful to his promises because he is faithful to himself. *Rahamim* means God's tender compassion. *Rahamim* ("compassion") comes from the Hebrew noun *rehem*, meaning "womb" or "uterus." Thus God's tender compassion is like the tender union between a pregnant mother and the child she protects and nourishes in her womb. John Paul II says this aspect of God as mother is perhaps best expressed in Isaiah 49:15: "Can a mother forget her infant, or be without tenderness for the child of her womb? Even should she forget you, I will never forget you."[38]

Judith MacNutt told us a story of how she experienced this motherly side of God. Judith had struggled for many years with fear and distrust of God. When Judith's daughter Rachel was born, Judith was overwhelmed with love for Rachel. One day as she held Rachel and nursed her, Judith began to cry with awe and joy over her love for Rachel. Then Judith heard God say, "You really love her, don't you?" Judith said, "Yes, so much." God said, "I love you more." Judith said, "No you don't." God said, "Yes I do, and I feel even more joy when I nourish you than you feel as you nurse your child." Judith told us that her fear of God was healed at that moment as, "Something so deep broke within me. God had to give me a child so that I could understand God's love." Thus God revealed herself to Judith as being more mother than the best of human mothers.

Positive and Negative Memories in the Stage of Trust

It's so easy to get hurt. Anyone who, like Judith, has a baby knows that babies are often cold or tired or hungry, and almost always wet. Hurts happen because mothers can't always come right away. But the good news is that it's even easier to have hurts healed than to have them happen.

How can we have hurts healed? First, we can return to positive memories and take in the ways Jesus and others loved us. Then, we can return to negative memories and bring Jesus into them.

We need to return to positive memories because we're loved with more love than we can receive at one time. We all know this from experiences of loving people who have not responded to us. I remember watching the birth of a baby. The mother was in labor for ten hours, and every cell of her body lovingly longed for the baby's arrival. But that baby came into the world screaming, hollering, and so focused on the trauma of birth that it missed all the love in the room. The baby didn't begin to take in love until the doctor placed it on the mother. For me that child's birth images how more love is offered than we can often receive. No matter how much emotional deprivation we have experienced, at least some love was given us or we would not have survived, but died of marasmus, like the orphaned babies without someone like Old Anna.

We can always go back later and receive the love that was given us. But what if we don't remember being loved, especially during this earliest stage of infancy? I (Matt) don't remember what happened to me when I was an infant. But I can look at photographs of my mother with her infant grandson, David. In those photographs, my mother is gazing into David's eyes with so much love. She holds him up in the air as if he were her whole world. David has probably added ten years to my mother's life. When my mother writes me a letter, it's usually one page . . . unless she's just seen David. Then it's three or four pages, because "There's no other child in the world with the IQ David has." Jesus loved me through my mother in the same way I see her loving David. I can keep returning to the image of the sparkle in her eyes as she holds David, and take in all the love she gave me as an infant. I can also return to other images of being loved in infancy: all those who stood around my crib and said I was as good-looking as my mother or as strong as my father, the way my father (who missed being drafted into World War II because of his flat feet) would hurry home from work each day to have lunch with me, and all my smiling baby pictures that show how loved I must have felt.

After we feel rooted in positive memories of how Jesus has loved us, we can return to negative memories and bring Jesus into them to heal our hurts. If you, like me, are a first child, you probably have some hurts that need healing because the first child is usually the guinea pig with whom parents make all their mistakes. Parents are more fearful and unsure of themselves with their first child, and so that child will usually turn out more fearful and serious than later children. The world of the first child is the parents, and so this child often absorbs more parental attitudes (both good and bad) and more parental fears of all that can go wrong. The first child is also often a perfectionist, since it is expected to be a responsible model for younger brothers and sisters. Other children may be hurt in different ways, such as the middle child who is overlooked or the younger child who is not allowed to grow up.[39]

When I return to negative memories for healing, I also recall that I was not breastfed, that my family had to eke their way through the depression, and they had me arrive just months after the lowest point of World War II, Pearl Harbor. Young children sense not only tension within the family, but they also sense tension in the larger world, as evidenced by the current epidemic of children having nightmares of atomic war.[40] For me, the greatest catastrophe of all was having to share my world with a brother who took the spotlight away from me when I was barely two years old. When I go back to that negative memory, where I have to share center stage and the whole focus is no longer on me, I climb up into the lap of Jesus (Mk. 10:13–15)—or sometimes into the lap of Mary or God my perfect Mother—where I am hugged tight and hear, "Can a mother forget her infant, be without tenderness for the child of her womb? Even should she forget, I will never forget you." (Is. 49:15)

Healing Infancy

One easy way to heal hurts from infancy is to join Jesus in the scene of his own birth. Jesus is so eager to share with us his experience of being loved as an infant that we don't even have to know what memory he wants to heal. A psychiatrist who works with schizophrenic children told us that she prays for these children to share Jesus' birth and to be held by Mary and Joseph in the stable at Bethlehem. As the children begin to experience the perfect love of a mother and a father, missing in their own early years, they stop hallucinating and their condition improves. We asked her how she had learned to pray for healing by going to Bethlehem. She said,

> That's how I was healed. I couldn't let people touch me. Whenever they tried, I felt like a fire alarm had gone off inside of me and I wanted to say, 'You can keep your distance. I don't want your sentimental paws all over me.' I knew I needed healing, but during all my years of psychoanalysis I was never able to find out why I resisted touch.* One day a friend agreed to pray with me and to ask Jesus to show us the memory. We were silent for ten minutes, and then when we shared with each other what we had seen, we

---

*Here and in other places in this book, we tell stories of people who came to us for prayer after psychotherapy had not brought them complete healing. This does not mean any lack of respect for psychotherapy on our parts; a psychotherapist might report opposite experiences, of clients who came to them for help after healing prayer had not brought them complete healing. With deep hurts, the ideal is a combination of healing prayer and psychotherapy. As resources for those who wish to integrate prayer and therapy, we recommend *The Journal of Christian Healing*, 103 Dudley Ave., Narberth, PA 19072 and the Association of Christian Therapists, 725 Bayview Ave., Clearwater, FL 34619-4217.

both had the same image. We both saw me as a
six-month-old baby, being held at Bethlehem.
During the next several weeks, I returned to this
image in my prayer many times. I couldn't seem
to get enough of being held by Joseph and Mary
as a six-month-old baby. I thought I should be
smaller, since at Bethlehem Jesus was only a new-
born. But if I tried to shrink myself down, as soon
as I focused on taking in love and forgot about
what size I was, I'd be back up to six months
again. After several weeks of prayer, I noticed
that I could let the children touch me without feeling like a fire alarm was going off inside me.
When I went home to visit my own mother, I said
to her, 'I don't understand why I'm praying this
way. Did anything happen to me when I was six
months old?' My mother said, 'When you were
six months old, you had a rash and you were covered with blisters. For several weeks I could not
hold you. It was so painful that we couldn't put
clothes on you, we couldn't bathe you—no one
could touch you at all.' Then I knew why I had to
be six months old in my prayer. It was at six
months that I first heard the message, 'touch is
painful,' and it was then that I most needed to
take in love.

Jesus knows where we need to be healed. We don't
even have to remember how we were hurt. Like our psychiatrist friend, all we have to do is go to where we're most
hungry for love and Jesus will meet us there. Each person
has been hurt differently and is healed differently. In giving retreats, we have noticed how each person prays
through the scene of Bethlehem in a different way. Some

go to Joseph to be held, and others who were never nursed become Mary's baby and are breastfed. Some who were hurt in the womb experience Mary taking them into her own womb, while those who long for a child may join Mary as she holds Jesus. All go where they most need to give and receive the love that will heal them.

The following prayer invites us to join Jesus at Bethlehem and receive love in whatever ways we most needed it before our birth or during our infancy.

Bethlehem Prayer

a. Picture the stable in Bethlehem where Jesus was born. Enter the scene with all your senses. See Mary and Joseph each in turn pick up Jesus and tenderly love him.

b. Let yourself take Jesus' place. Let Mary hold you and fill you up with all the love your mother was unable to give you from the time you first came into her womb. Then let Joseph's strong hands cradle you and fill you up with the love and security your father was unable to give. You may wish to see your own parents standing next to Mary and Joseph.

Chapter 2:

Early Childhood
(Autonomy vs. Shame and Doubt)

Who Is in Control?

Melvin, an absent-minded monk, took a daily walk to read his breviary. Unfortunately, Easter Sunday had extra psalms to read and Melvin walked too far—right off a cliff. Fortunately, he felt something was amiss and grabbed a tree branch. As Melvin's feet dangled three hundred feet over the canyon, he frantically shouted,
"Help! Is there anyone up there?"
Suddenly the clouds parted and a loud voice boomed,
"I will help you. Are you willing to do whatever I ask?"
"Of course. What do you want me to do?"
"Let go."
"Who are you?"
"God."
"Is there anyone else up there?"

[Unknown]

Anyone around a two-year-old knows that child's favorite words: "no," "my," "mine," "I." At the bottom of the list is "yes." From eighteen months to three years roughly is the "no" stage. Erikson appropriately calls this the stage of autonomy vs. shame and doubt. Autonomy develops as the child tries to develop its own will and get what it wants. Shame develops as a child chooses its own will and experiences the disappointment of its mother and others for not living up to their expectations.[1] In choosing its own will, the child is not trying to disconnect from mother, but rather seeking a separate sense of self so that it can relate to her in whole new ways.[2] (See Chapter 5, pages 135–137 and footnote #24.)

Remember When You Were Two?

I (Matt) remember when my sister, Mary Ellen, was going this stage. Being the oldest child in the family, I was the one who was always asked to do all the work around the house. So, my mother would say to me, "Go help Mary Ellen clean up her room," which translated meant, "Go clean up Mary Ellen's room." Because as soon as I would say, "Mary Ellen, would you pick up your room?", she would say, "No!" So I had to be very sneaky about this and figure out how a two-year-old's mind works. I'd say, "Mary Ellen, we've got these dolls all over. Whose dolls are these?" And she would say, "Mine!" And I'd say, "Oh, mine! They're mine. Oh good, then I get to pick them up. Don't you dare touch them." And she'd say,

"No, they're mine!" Then she'd go running around and pick up all her dolls. You have to think like a two-year-old to survive a two-year-old.

The reason that two-year-old's are becoming their own person is they are learning many new things. They are learning how to walk, they can stand on their own two feet and feel important, go where they want. They are learning to talk; usually they have from twenty to two hundred words by two years of age. They can sit comfortably and they can discard things. Any mother who has fed a two-year-old knows how that works. They are beginning to have control over their own body. This is the stage of toilet training. It's the stage when a toddler will walk around with that malodorous lump in its britches and say, "I didn't do it." They will blush as they say that, because they have a sense of shame.

The child's capacity for shame can easily be exploited by harsh parents, or it can be lovingly guided by sensitive parents. When the three of us visited Steve and Mary's home for the first time, they prepared a special outdoor barbeque meal for us and invited two other friends of ours to join the celebration. As we all gathered around the picnic table, we noticed Steve's four-year-old daughter, Alicia, squatting down in a corner of the yard. As she saw us look at her, Alicia's face blushed with shame. We knew by her posture and her face that she was wetting her pants. Alicia knew that we knew. Steve quietly said to us, "She's very regressed right now. She's not used to this many new people in her home at once." Then Steve picked Alicia up and gently carried her inside the house. A few minutes later, he carried her back outside. He had washed her and put a clean dress on her—an especially pretty, feminine dress. Steve knew that Alicia's fear had caused her to temporarily regress emotionally from age four to age two, and that she already felt enough shame over her immature be-havior. He cared more about her than about looking good in front of guests by having a "perfect" child. Rather than exploit her shame by scolding her for making a mess, Steve's loving care said to Alicia, "You're still my pretty daughter and I love you, no matter what."

How Do You Create Healthy Autonomy?

Affirmation, such as Steve gave his daughter, is what a child needs for development in the stage of autonomy. It needs to be affirmed in the ways that will bring forth its will healthily. That means whenever it's making the right choices, to really approve those choices. Psychologists find that even from nine to eighteen months, the child learns the basis of autonomy if it is given the initiative in games at least 30–40% of the time.[3] Likewise those who are com-fortable with all their emotions and have empathy with the child also help the child choose to express its full emotional range.[4] So all the people who rejoiced when you chose for them to read "The Three Little Pigs," and then pretended to be frightened by the wolf and thrilled as the pigs stood up to him—those were the people who really built your will, the ones that helped you decide and come into being.

But it also takes not just affirmation of the right choices, it takes the whole inner part of that word: firm. It takes firmness when there's the wrong choice. When the child is turning on all the gas burners and then putting his hand in them just to see what happens, it takes the firm-ness to say "No," even though that child is going to go back and try it again and try it again. He has to test his will against yours. It takes that firmness so that the child learns that there are some things that he just can't choose. Otherwise, the child will grow up to be a dictator. He will be a little Hitler, and the whole family will have to respond to every single dictate that he has. He becomes the adult who has to get his own way.

Failure to achieve the right balance between love and firmness is easily passed on from one generation to the next. Our friends Andy (a psychotherapist) and Karen told us that they both came from homes where they were not given enough loving attention. Thus, when their first child, Susan, was born, they were determined she would receive as much love as possible. So, when Susan cried rather than fall asleep, Andy and Karen held her long into the night. They found that Susan fell asleep faster if there was a steady background noise such as a vacuum cleaner while they carried and rocked her. Within a short time, Susan wouldn't go to sleep unless she was carried with a rocking motion while the vacuum cleaner ran. Finally, Andy and Karen realized that Susan was programming them rather than learning autonomy from them. Andy and Karen had failed to model healthy autonomy for Susan because they had not respected their own needs for sleep. In exhausted desperation, they gave Susan "the treatment." They were lovingly present to her at bedtime, but once Susan was in her crib, Andy and Karen refused to pick her up again. After several nights of tears and tantrums, Susan learned to fall asleep on her own. Looking back now, Andy and Karen tell us they regret "the treatment," since the sudden deprivation of being held at bedtime was too harsh and traumatic an adjustment for Susan. Instead, they wish they had very gradually reduced the amount of time they spent holding Susan at bedtime.

By the time Andy and Karen's second child, David, was born, they were much more secure themselves and had a healthy sense of autonomy. They picked David up often and held him when he cried, but communicated to David that their limits needed to be respected. David never made the excessive demands at bedtime that Susan had made. Although it is possible that Susan and David are simply different in their needs for attention, Andy told us, "I think David was different because *we* were different." Susan had become more and more disturbed by her parents' failure to respect their own needs, while David sensed the healthy autonomy in his parents and peacefully respected their limits. As Alice Miller writes,

> A child who has been breast-fed for nine months and no longer wants to drink from the breast does not have to be taught to give it up. And a child who has been allowed to be egoistic, greedy, and asocial long enough will develop spontaneous pleasure in sharing and giving. . . . If a mother respects both herself and her child from his very first day onward, she will never need to teach him respect for others. He will, of course, take both himself and others seriously—he couldn't do otherwise. But a mother who, as a child, was herself not taken seriously by her mother as the person she really was will crave this respect from her child as a substitute; and she will try to get it by training him to give it to her.[5]

Parents who themselves have a healthy ability to say "yes" and "no" are likely to naturally find the right balance between overpermissiveness and harsh firmness, and thus create healthy autonomy in their children.

No Will—No Protection from Future Hurts

While Andy and Karen erred on the side of being too permissive with Susan, the more common error is that the will of the child gets stamped out by a parent being too firm, and constantly saying no, so that the child never makes her own choices. This opens the child up to many hurts. Psychologist Martin Seligman says the main factor in whether a person gets permanently hurt or not doesn't seem to be the severity of the situation. People go through tremendous crises—deaths, prison camps, murders, rapes—and they can grow from them. Others get wiped out by just a minor thing. They fall down the stairs and for the rest of their life they're afraid of everything. According to Dr. Seligman, it isn't the severity of the situation, but whether people feel helpless and out of control. If they don't sense that they have a will, that they're in charge, then anything can just come in and wipe them out.[6] That's why this stage is so important. It builds that inner resiliency. Because I have a self, I can bounce back on my own two feet. Nothing is going to wipe me out. With my will I can say no to all the ways a situation is paralyzing me and begin to grow by making the choices I can make rather than be passively dependent on the situation to change.

A healthy will fosters physical and emotional health. Many believe that dependency illnesses (addictions) have roots in a wounded sense of autonomy. Seligman finds that 70% of physical illness strikes when a person is feeling helpless or hopeless—powerless to choose and be in autonomous control.[7] For example, those with a "hardy personality" (who believe they can exert some influence over events and who welcome change for the opportunities it brings) even react to stress with a lower rise in diastolic blood pressure and have healthier hearts.[8] The professions with the highest rate of heart disease are those with no control over stress—telephone operators, cooks, cashiers and assembly line workers—in contrast to low heart disease among lawyers and managers who can control their own schedules and interruptions.[9]

But whether you are a lawyer or a telephone operator, the crisis of autonomy, like each of Erikson's stages, is not totally resolved in the toddler but continues through a lifetime. For example, in a dysfunctional family, such as an alcoholic home, the child experiences not autonomy but confusion and shame in the chaos. Even into adult life, children may assume any of four roles to survive. Often the "hero," or caretaker, usually the oldest child, becomes a surrogate parent by supervising the other children and running the household. This "hero" is often a superachiever in studies or athletics. In contrast, the "scapegoat" or problem child misbehaves to draw attention away from the alcoholism or to express family tension. The "mascot" tries to minimize the problems by joking, clowning and pretending to be carefree. Finally, the "lost child" fades into the background in an attempt to withdraw from the turmoil.[10]

If a parent has healthily resolved his own crisis of autonomy, he can help his children resolve theirs, as does the father of the prodigal son. In the story of the prodigal son (Lk. 15:11–32), both the elder brother and the younger prodigal are struggling for autonomy by asking for their inheritance before their father is dead. "In fact, in all of Middle Eastern literature (aside from the prodigal story) from ancient times to the present, there is no case of any son, older or younger, asking for his inheritance from a father who is still in good health."[11] In doing so, the sons are committing the worst "unthinkable" crime because they are treating their father as if he were dead. But the father trusts both sons and treats them in opposite ways. He does not confront the prodigal but permits him the freedom to go off and make mistakes with the inheritance. Yet in an atmosphere of trust where "everything I have is yours," the father does confront the mistakes of his eldest son. Tough love that confronts one son will destroy another son who needs his freedom affirmed. Only a loving, trusting heart knows whether permissive love or tough love is best for each person. Struggles with autonomy resolve themselves to the degree that the love is deep and recognized as love rather than as a contest of wills.

Autonomy and Our Image of God

Those struggling with autonomy not only struggle to relate to people but also to God. We can overuse our will and become a dictator to God or underuse our will and be a smiling Mona Lisa with no desires. Many who pray for healing dictate to God with an arm-twisting prayer. It's almost as if they feel they have to change God's will. "God, you promised to heal this person. This person is in great need (long sob story follows). I quote to you your promises. You have to keep your promises." That's dictation. That isn't respecting God's will—how much God loves and wants to heal that person. I don't have to have faith in my will's faith. I should have faith in God's will, in God's love being even greater than mine.

The opposite of being a dictator is to be a perpetually smiling Mona Lisa with no will who never gives God the real feelings, the real desires. The fear is that if I ask God specifically for what I really want, it is going to be immoral, illegal or fattening, so why bother. Just smile, pray in general terms, praise the Lord, and don't reveal my own desires or I'll be disappointed or they may be wrong. I am ashamed of my negative feelings so I hide these too from God and myself. I hide my will rather than do as St. Ignatius and other masters of prayer teach—trust my desires and ask for what I want. If I just come with, "Well Jesus, anything that you want is fine," not as much happens. I don't grow in my desire for Jesus to act. Gradually I find I don't desire to pray because prayer is removed from my deepest desires.

But when I pray with my deepest desires, I discover as Jesus did in the agony in the garden that my deepest desires are God's desires. "Father, if it is possible let all this pass from me. At first glance, I can't go through this. Yet, not my will but yours be done. When I get to the core of my heart, I know that the desires I will discover are the same as those you have had for me all along." At this stage, prayer of petition such as Jesus prayed in the agony in the garden heals to the extent that, like Jesus, we move through our surface desires and pray with our deepest desires. Discerning our desires with the Spiritual Exercises of St. Ignatius and with a spiritual director can further clarify our deepest desires to do God's will.[12]

Praying in tongues is also very helpful to express the Spirit's desires. Her desires go beyond the limits of words (Rm. 8:26). During a retreat we attended with eighty other Jesuit priests, all received the gift of tongues because it was so needed by these priests who had developed their intellectual side more than their feeling side. After singing in tongues, the Jesuits renewed their vows. They did so with newly freed desires to do God's will with their whole heart and not just with their whole mind (Mt. 22:37). Petition and the renewing of our deepest commitments heals the wounded will if it builds upon trust in God's love (Erikson's first stage). If not, the focus of prayer should be on

positive memories of God's love, especially during the
stage of autonomy, until we want to love God because God
has first loved us. The sign of a healed will is the movement
from I *should* love God to I *want to* love because God loves
me so much. Renewing of the will's commitment (e.g.,
vows, baptismal promises, altar calls) is important, but the
best time to renew the will's commitment is after we know
the first stage's trust in a God of love and spontaneously
want to give ourselves to such a lover. Thus, what we
sometimes call "willpower" might better be called "love
power" since the power to act lovingly usually happens to
the degree we have allowed ourselves to take in love.

Positive and Negative Memories in the Stage of Autonomy

Perhaps the easiest question to help us recall memories in this stage is: who during these years expressed and
helped us express the full range of positive and negative
emotions? Or, who could say "yes" and "no" to us in a
loving way? A story about my dad puts those questions
most into perspective for me. I (Dennis) never did like
canned vegetables, especially peas. So I can remember as
a child saying, "I'm not going to eat my peas." And my dad
would say, "You *are* going to eat your peas. I will help
you." And finally, he would make a game of it. So, he'd
take a spoon and he'd start playing airplane, circling the
spoon around in the air until it was ready to land in the
runway of my mouth. But what saved my dad is that he
had a variation of airplane. One spoon for him and one for
myself. I figured that I was really getting a good deal because I only had to eat half the peas. I never figured out
that dad probably dished me up twice as many peas as he

expected me to eat. What I appreciate now as I look back on those episodes is that my father not only said, "No, you have to eat your peas," but also "Yes, I will help you." That gift of both "yes" and "no" has helped me say both strong "yes's" and strong "no's." For instance, the three of us spend forty weeks each year traveling. If we go to a country for a month, we tell people that we'll work only half of the time, for fifteen of those days. So we say "yes" to them for half of it and "no" to them for the other half. The other half we take for ourselves, to read, write and rest. Despite much traveling during the past thirteen years, I have not missed even one complete day because of sickness. My dad's gift of saying "yes" and "no" has helped me live at a healthy pace.

When I look back on my early life and try to recall the time when I felt my ability to say "yes" and "no" was hurt most, it was my third Christmas. I can remember as a little kid going to see Santa Claus. I never could figure out how Santa Claus knew my name. I never knew that my dad said, "Santa Claus, you know Dennis don't you?" And Santa Claus would say, "Dennis! How are you?" And I would just go, "My gosh, Santa knows my name." One time after seeing Santa Claus my dad took me into the washroom. When I was coming out of the washroom, I followed the wrong set of legs. I was in a sixteen-story building and had climbed a lot of stairs before I looked up those legs and saw that it wasn't my dad. I can remember the howl I let out. The startled owner of that set of legs swooped me up and sat me on a stack of rugs. So I sat on that stack of rugs as I cried all the louder for my daddy. Luckily my mother had pinned a large name tag on me with my phone number, so eventually they called her at home. She finally located my dad and told him to head upstairs to the rug department. But it seemed forever before my dad finally arrived. During that time I felt I had not only lost my dad but also my autonomy, and that my power to make decisions had been taken from me. I felt like a child locked in a house with no key and no way of getting out.

After that Christmas episode, I frequently had fear of being locked in. So I wouldn't go into movie theaters or stores. Or if we were in a gas station getting the car filled with gas and someone went inside to get refreshments, I'd stay in our car so I wouldn't get locked inside the gas station. In many ways I still have fear of being locked in. For example, in planning a conference or in accepting invitations, I don't like to plan too far ahead. This makes it difficult for people who work with me and want to know what the conference will be about before we walk out on the stage, or for people who send an invitation and need a prompt answer so that they can find someone else if I say "no." I'm always hoping for something better to come along and afraid to get locked into a situation I can't change. I still fear my autonomy being taken away, of being locked in and unable to say "yes" or "no."

What if you can't remember any early hurts? Sometimes it helps to look at childhood photos and see if a memory fits a facial expression you see in a photo of yourself. Or, imagine yourself as a two-year-old—throwing food, spilling milk, breaking something or hitting another child. Then imagine your parents and how they respond to you. Although you may not be actually remembering real events, the feelings and attitudes you experience as you imagine such scenes *are* real and they express the way your heart remembers what your conscious mind may have forgotten. Another way to get in touch with how your heart may need healing is to ask yourself how you react now to a two-year-old throwing food, spilling milk, etc. What would you say or do? If you would react with "Be more careful!'' or "Shame on you!,'' ask yourself who may have shouted something similar at you. What is your earliest memory of being corrected or punished? Whom did you feel most distant from in your family—a sibling rival, an alcoholic or absent parent? When was the first time you recall being unhappy? We don't have to uncover the deepest hurts, but simply let Jesus' love touch the pain of any real or imaginary hurtful scenes.

Healing Early Childhood

In many cases childhood hurts can be healed as soon as they happen. We can pray for a child without the child's participation, as Barbara prayed for Jennifer (Chapter 1). Even a small child old enough to talk can participate in a simple prayer for healing. One wise mother told us how she prayed for her son, Michael. When Michael was in the autonomy stage, he found his baby brother dead in his crib one morning. Michael loved his roommate brother and was heartbroken. Two years later, five-year-old Michael was refusing to go to school. Since he was doing well in school and had many friends, Michael's mother knew there must be something else bothering him. She was led to take Michael back to the scene of his brother's death.

"Mike, can you see your bedroom and Jesus in the corner?''
"Yes.''
"Let Jesus take you over to the crib and show you Tom the morning you found him dead. What is Jesus saying and doing?''
"Jesus has his hand on my shoulder and he is sad.

He says Tom died not because of anything I did
but because he wasn't made right."
"Do you fear that I too might die or get hurt if you
go to school?"
"Yes."
"What does Jesus say?"
"He says he will never leave me."

From that day on, Michael went to school with no fear. He
was no longer stuck in the stage of autonomy but was now
free to say "no" to the fear of his mother abandoning him
and "yes" to going to school.

Michael's mother was able to pray with him as a child,
so that he would not have to carry his hurt into adulthood.
But often no one is there to pray with us at the time we are
hurt, and those hurts shape our later development. Fortunately, it is never too late to pray for healing for ourselves
or for another.

When I (Sheila) recall the autonomy stage and think of
a person who said "no" to me, one of the people I think of
is my mother. When my mother said "no," she would add,
"I am going to break your will." My mother conveyed to
me that my will was bad and that I did not have the right
to say "yes" or "no." My mother did this because she had
a serious illness that affected her both emotionally and
physically. One symptom of her illness was that she lacked
the quality of empathy which enables us to get inside of
another person's shoes and see their needs as different
from ours. Because my mother couldn't see the difference
between another person and herself, she didn't feel guilt
or remorse when she hurt others by trespassing on their
needs or violating their will.

I had not only a mentally ill mother, but also healthy
and loving grandparents with whom I spent much of my

childhood. So, some of my experience at this stage was healthy. But still, those words of my mother and the attitude behind them of "I am going to break your will," did affect me very deeply. I grew up with difficulty in asserting myself. I could force myself to be assertive if something I really believed in was at stake, but not without considerable fear and guilt, especially if I was opposing another person. Usually I seemed very timid, but at other times I would try so hard to be assertive that I would seem overly insistent, all the while feeling frightened inside. I got over some of this struggle to be assertive as I grew up, through feeling loved by God and others and learning to trust my desires as basically good. But I still struggled often to express assertiveness in healthy ways.

The Turning Point

The greatest turning point in that struggle came a few years ago when I visited my parents during a family crisis. My mother's illness often caused her to treat my father in abusive ways. But when I arrived to visit them, I saw that what had been an unhappy situation had become a life-threatening one for my father. He had developed ulcerative colitis, a stress-related illness that can come from keeping things in. He had gone from 180 lbs. down to 116 lbs., had symptoms of malnutrition, and was so weak he couldn't walk more than ten feet without collapsing. He was unable to care for himself. My mother was not only unable to care for him, but she was preventing him from getting the care he needed from a doctor.

Although I saw how serious the situation was, I doubted if anything could be done to help my parents. No one had ever been able to intervene in their situation before and I didn't think I would be able to do any better. But I knew I had to at least try. I asked Jesus to give me whatever I needed: courage, more love, etc. Then I went to my mother and I tried to tell her my father was very seriously ill. (Later, I found out that he would have died within a few months if he hadn't gotten medical care.) My mother began to scream, "No, no," and I began to feel frightened and guilty just as I had in childhood when I asked her for anything. As an adult, I could see that I was asking for something reasonable. But part of me was still frightened.

I kept trying to explain the situation to my mother, but I was getting nowhere and feeling increasingly frightened. Then suddenly something happened that I had never experienced before. I felt a wave of pure feeling go through me. At first I didn't know what it was and I had to stop and try to identify what I felt. I realized what I was feeling was hatred, pure hatred.

I didn't know what to do and I tried to pray and listen to Jesus. I thought he might want to forgive me for my feeling of hatred, or ask me to forgive my mother. But as I listened to Jesus I heard something that surprised me, something very different from what I expected to hear. I heard Jesus say,

"Your hatred of evil is *my* hatred of evil.
When you say 'no' to evil it is *my* 'no' to evil."

I realized that Jesus was feeling pure hatred with me. It was not hatred for my mother. It was hatred for the illness in her that had damaged her life and was damaging our family. From that moment on, I was different. I was able to go ahead and do what was necessary to provide medical care for my father, despite my mother's objections. I took my father to the hospital and he had surgery. He recovered well and today he is healthier in many ways than ever before in his life.

I think that in this experience Jesus answered my prayers for help by giving me his healthy will and his sense of autonomy. He helped me use that sense of autonomy as it's meant to be used: to resist what is harmful for ourselves or for another, and to obtain what is good, that which God wants us to have. We can know what God means us to have by listening to our own deepest desires. Jesus helped me trust my deepest desires and learn how to say "yes" and "no" in the ways that he would say "yes" and "no." That gift of autonomy has stayed with me, and I find in my present life that I'm much more able to be assertive when necessary and say "yes" or "no" without fear or guilt as with Jesus I resist what is bad for me or for another and seek what is good.

Following is a prayer to help us grow in Jesus' healthy sense of autonomy, so we can say "yes" and "no" with him.

Agony in the Garden Prayer

a. Make a fist with your hand. Feel the tension in it, and ask Jesus to show you one area of your life where you feel tension or want change. Experience how Jesus within you shares your tension, especially if it blocks you from giving and receiving love.

b. Join Jesus in the Garden of Gethsemane, as he feels tension over situations that block giving and receiving love. Repeat with Jesus his words, "Father, if it be possible, let this pass from me." Repeat these words several times until you can say them with the same intensity as Jesus does. As you say them, breathe deeply and take in from Jesus the power to change what you can change.

c. Then repeat with Jesus his words, "Yet not my will but yours be done." As you say these words several times, open your hands and breathe the situation out into Jesus' hands. Breathe in from Jesus the strength to endure those situations which will not change.*

---

*Caution: Beware of praying this prayer to accept a physical or emotional illness. Normally we can assume that it *is* God's will to heal us so we can be free to give and receive more love.

Chapter 3

Play Age
(Initiative vs. Guilt)

The Clergyman Who Was All Wet

There was once a clergyman who lived in a town that was hit by a major flood. The water was a foot deep in his living room. Some parishioners in a boat rowed up to his door, asking him to join them. "No, go ahead," the clergyman replied. "I'll be just fine. God is taking care of me." So they left.

Then the water rose to the second floor. Back came his anxious parishioners in the boat. Again they asked him to join them. Again he refused.

By the time the boat came back once more, the house had been completely engulfed and the clergyman was standing on his chimney. "Reverend," his parishioners called to him, "come with us! You'll drown."

"No," the clergyman replied. "I'll be fine. The Lord is providing."

So they left. And he drowned.

Later, in heaven, the clergyman angrily made an appointment to see God. "Why did you do this to me?" the clergyman fumed. "I did what you said. I prayed. And you didn't help me."

"Didn't help you?" God answered in surprise. "What do you mean? I sent a boat around to get you three times."

[Toby Rice Drews, *Getting Them Sober II*]

When I (Dennis) say I'm working hard, frequently Matt and Sheila will say, "Dennis, you're hardly working!" But that's also what makes me an authority on Erikson's third stage of "initiative," otherwise referred to as the stage of play. During this stage (ages 3–5), children possess a "surplus of energy," allowing them to become "self-activated" or "initiators," especially as they master three skills: language, movement and imagination.[1] Since these three skills help children intrude on the boundaries of the adult world, this stage is also called the stage of intrusion. Thus children master new ways of intruding with language and of saying, "Give me this," or "Give me that." Children also intrude by movement as they climb up to reach things that even parents thought were out of reach.

Children intrude especially through their imagination because they can become whatever they imagine themselves to be. For myself, this was the age of cowboys and Indians. Matt and I had a tent in the backyard. From the tent we could take careful aim at the imaginary Indians who were shooting their bows and arrows from behind the picket fence. The Indians always got shot. I never did. Fifteen years later when I worked on the Sioux Indian reservation and some of my closest friends were Indians, I marveled at the power of a child's imagination which could make me into a "good guy" and the Indians into "bad guys."

Since imagination is a key to understanding this stage, you might want to imagine the following playful scene and watch what you would say and do.

Imagine yourself about three years old and in your

kitchen. Can you remember your kitchen table? Walk up to it. How high up do you come to the kitchen table? Are you neck level, a little taller, a little smaller?

Then eye the cupboard. Imagine you know that in the cupboard are some candy bars hidden away. Perhaps your mother hid them for your upcoming birthday party or for Christmas. All mothers have secret hiding places known only to children. Shove a stool (maybe the stool is as tall as you are) over to the cupboard. Then climb up there. As you balance on your tiptoes, grasp the cupboard with one hand and reach for the candy with the other hand. Imagine that as you grab the candy, your hand accidentally hits your mother's best teacup. The cup crashes to the floor and splits into tiny pieces.

What happens now? What do you do with the candy bars in your hand? What about the cup? How do you decide to handle the situation with your mother? How does your mother react?

If you are like me, you probably didn't eat the candy bars and you probably tried to clean up the mess so your mother wouldn't find out. Not only did I put the candy back in the exact spot from which I had taken it, but I also cleaned up the cup pieces and threw them in the bottom of the wastebasket. Then I went outside and started to play in the tent. Pretty soon I heard my mother call, "Den-nis." To prepare for this emergency, I had picked a bouquet of dandelions. As I handed her the dandelions, I put on my innocent face and asked with wonderment, "What, Mom?" She said, "Dennis, what are these chips doing here?" (How come there is always evidence that only a mother can see?) So I said to her, "Mom, I was going to get you a cup of tea. When I reached up for one of your cups, it just kinda fell down." Then she said, "Dennis, what should you do when something breaks?" (That's a mother question you don't answer. You just give the puzzled look.) "Dennis, anytime you break something, you're supposed to come and tell me. Now what will you do if something breaks again?" "Oh, I'll come and tell you, Mom." And finally I imagined her saying, "Dennis, I want you to be more careful around my dishes. If you can be real careful, I'd like you to help me set the table right now." And I said to myself, "Wow, the pressure is off. I'll set as many tables as you want!"

Now I don't know if that's the way my mother would actually respond. But it is the way I pictured it. Whatever the response, this imagination exercise suggests several important developments at this stage. First, as already mentioned, you become what you imagine. And so you can make up all kinds of stories, such as about making a cup of tea for your mother. Your wonderful imagination triggers playfulness and initiative as you set out to explore everything from the top cupboard shelf to the bottom of the wastebasket. But whether your healthy playfulness, curiosity and initiative continue to develop depends, according to Erikson, on a critical factor in this stage: the management of guilt. A capacity for guilt comes from an emerging conscience. You know something is wrong even if no one tells you it's wrong. You don't have to count on public opinion (shame) to know that you'd better clean up that broken cup.

Developing Guilt

Children are so sensitive to guilt at this stage that not only will they probably feel guilty about breaking a cup, but they also may feel totally responsible and guilty for things they had little or nothing to do with, such as their parents' divorce or even the death of a friend. Because of this oversensitivity, children scolded continually with such words as "bad girl" or "bad boy" may end up with deep self-hatred. This happens because children are often unable to distinguish between their person being "bad" as opposed to only their action being "bad."

Thus crippling or unhealthy guilt would result any-time children perceive criticism or punishment to mean that they themselves are bad. Crippling or unhealthy guilt results when a child not only hates the sin (e.g., causing a breakdown in mother's trust by not honestly reporting a broken cup) but also *hates the sinner* (i.e., child hates himself); whereas healthy guilt results when the child hates the sin but *loves the sinner.* Being told I am a "bad boy," along with a spanking to emphasize the point, can change my *behavior* and may keep me out of the cupboard as well as keep me from breaking another cup. But while fear of punishment and triggering unhealthy guilt can change the *behavior* of a child (or anyone else over whom we have influence), such fear and guilt can't change the *child,* at least not to become loving. Only love can make a child loving. If through a punishment I perceive myself as a bad or unloving person (i.e., I feel unhealthy guilt about who I am), continued use of such punishment will probably create self-hatred and make me unloving.[2]

Signs of children's unhealthy guilt and self-hatred vary: children will either become excessively angry at themselves (repressed self-hatred) or excessively angry at others (self-hatred projected outward). Signs of repressed unhealthy guilt and self-hatred introjected range from depression to perfectionism. In depression with its gloom and discouragement, I do not try to hide my self-hatred; whereas in perfectionism I try to do all the right things in hopes I can hide my self-hatred and once again feel good about myself. In such perfectionism, I become a pharisee, trying to keep the letter of the law so that I (and unconsciously my parent or whoever punished me) may once again feel good about myself. Driven for years by unhealthy guilt, the perfectionist's strained body often becomes victim to psychosomatic illness, while the perfectionist's spirit frequently becomes victim to scruples, often in matters of sexuality or work.

When children's unhealthy guilt and self-hatred are projected outward at others, the target will usually be the parent or whoever else punished them. Thus when children grow older and more able, they will frequently punish their parents by acting in ways that displease the parents—and often even end up punishing others, especially their own children.[3]

Unfortunately punishment affects not only how children will continue to relate to their parents, but also to God. At this stage, because of their sheer size and power, parents are like God. As Erikson says, through the voice of the parent, the child "now hears, as it were, God's voice without seeing God."[4] Thus, in an atmosphere of punishment that teaches the child to hate the sin *and* the sinner, that child may continually feel like the sinner in the hands of an angry God and grow up wondering what punishment God is going to inflict next.

What Heals Unhealthy Guilt?

If hating the sin and loving the sinner is so important, what would have helped me experience that? For me, to have hated the sin would have meant to experience the pain I caused my mother not only by breaking her best cup but, more importantly, by breaking the bond of trust between us. To have loved myself as sinner, I would have had to know that my mother loved me even though she didn't love what I did. Strengthened by her love, I would have had to own up to what I did, allow my mother to forgive me, and extend that forgiveness to myself. If I had done all these steps, I could have experienced healthy guilt and a God who, with me, could hate my sin and yet love me as sinner so I could change.

Although many reasons may exist for a child's extreme sensitivity to guilt at this stage, Freud suggested the Oedipal theory. According to this theory, a child's excessive guilt is a result of fantasies and desires to act out sexually with the parent of the opposite sex. Such Oedipal wishes, according to Freud, find expression in the boy's assurance that he will marry his mother and make her proud, and the girl's assurance that she will marry her father and take much better care of him than her mother does. Although children do desire at this time to bond themselves to their parents, especially to the parent of the opposite sex, many people question the Oedipal theory. We and they believe this theory applies mainly to dysfunctional families where unhealthy parents (not the children) with unmet sexual (and other) needs try to fulfill those needs through their children. The child then feels guilt and confusion at taking the place of the same-sex parent, a role it does not really want.[5]

Although the Oedipal theory may be inadequate, what seems correct is the child's desire at this stage to bond closely with parents. Much creative initiative and playfulness come from children's attempts to be like their parents. Thus while I would try to imitate my father's strength by carrying two very heavy shopping bags of groceries, my sister would try to imitate my mother's beauty by tripping around in my Mom's high heels. My identification with my father does not mean I ceased to need my mother. In a healthy family, the mother reveals the father to the child and the father reveals the mother. In the presence of my mother, my father became fully alive, and as she admired the tomatoes he had grown or told him all the things she loved about him, both he and I learned what it means to be a man. In this stage, as in all the stages, what a child needs most is not one parent or the other, but the loving union between them.

In trying to become like their parents, children begin to make comparisons between themselves and their parents. Children can begin to feel inadequate as they compare their size, intelligence, sexual capacity, or capacity to work with that of their parents. Thus children are extraordinarily appreciative of any ways they share or become more equal with parents, ways that assure them that someday they can be like their mother or father. And so simple things such as my mother allowing me to set the table with her or my father allowing me to put things into his shopping cart are crucially important. They give hope to the dream behind all the child's playful initiatives in this stage: the hope of becoming an adult just like Mom or Dad.

Positive and Negative Memories in the Stage of Initiative

I (Matt) needed much healing of this stage since for years I looked at play as an activity that revived me for the real goal of life: work. It seldom occurred to me to take a vacation, and a free day on our schedule seemed like a wasted day to me. I had few artistic talents and I read books to learn new things but seldom read a novel or poetry just to enjoy it. But in the last five years, I have found healing happening so that now I enjoy playing in some way daily, have dreamed up many of our recent vacations, and am more sensitive to beauty in music, color, flowers and poetry. Healing came gradually as I recalled memories of the play age and basked in the positive memories while bringing the Lord's love into the negative ones.

Healing came as first I recalled my positive play age memories: those who read to me and helped me imagine Santa landing on the roof, those who praised my artistic coloring and didn't notice when I went outside the lines, those who said "Try it." At age three, I was probably the only kid in our neighborhood with a library card, already researching my unanswered questions such as, "Where does the light go when the switch is turned off?" My mother and father encouraged me to swim, fish, ice skate, go sledding and build impregnable snow forts (and fearlessly defend them against waves of attacking Indians). I was the shortest kid on the block but every year my dad would say, "You can make the basketball team." So each year I'd try again for the team and last about two days before they would say, "Shorty, what are you doing out for this team? Try the girls' team!" I would return home and my mom would say, "You'll make it next year. You can do anything you put your mind to." I always felt encouraged to try anything and my healing deepens as I return to soak in these positive memories of being loved by parents who believed in me.

After soaking in my positive memories, I can explore my negative memories too. Children in the play age may be wounded deeply by hurts that choke their initiative to explore: too much time spent passively watching television, uprooting moves, hospitalizations, being hurt by a neighborhood bully or a dog, and anything that creates nightmares (thank God I only had Martians knocking on my window rather than all the Star Wars creatures and nuclear nightmares disturbing the present generation of children). Anything that creates guilt (e.g., sexual experiences, or being unable to resolve family conflicts) also chokes initiative.

My earliest memory of being unable to explore is spending ten painful, lonely days in a hospital while I had leg surgery. My earliest memory of feeling guilty is climbing up on a glass end table to get something and then crashing through shattering glass as the top gave way. I can still hear my mother shouting, "What business do you have being up there! Only your guardian angel kept you from hurting yourself!" (Then why didn't my angel keep me from getting up on the table too?) I also go back to other times of guilt that came later. My dad sent my dog Spot to live on a farm because, "You aren't taking care of him and the city is no place to keep a dog fenced up." In each of these memories, I reexperience the pain and then let Jesus be with me in the way I need him most.

Often even little hurts still have a big effect and may have to be reexperienced several times with Jesus. My mother used to send us out to ice skate in the Minneapolis winter, even when the mercury dipped below −10 degrees. Because we could go in and out of the warming house, skating was about the only sport possible when it got so cold. I grew to love warming houses and hated to hear, "You should go out and skate now." To this day I still don't like skating and react negatively to any suggestion that begins with, "You should go out and . . . " Each time I invite Jesus to be with me in my memories of ice skating, I am more free to choose my recreation and do it not because I should but because I want to. Before I jogged because I should jog to stay healthy. Now I jog because I enjoy jogging, admiring the exploding fall leaves and later soaking up a long hot shower.

While healing negative memories can free me to play in the present, playing with Jesus in the present can also heal negative memories. During my thirty day retreat, my retreat director encouraged me to play basketball every day. Because I love basketball and am only 5' 3", I compete fiercely to make up for my lack of height. Consequently I have an abundance of negative memories: being kicked off teams, chosen last, breaking my hand on a rebound, having my shots blocked by giants, and always being on the losing team. During the retreat I went home from basketball each day and shared with Jesus, letting him love me as I am—only 5' 3". Gradually I played not to do well but to enjoy it. Even when I missed shots and rebounds I could laugh at myself. I also took time to listen to music, garden, do artistic welding—things I really enjoy doing. My best prayer was often at the beginning of the day when I would ask, "What would I enjoy doing with Jesus?," and then do it. The more I enjoyed being with Jesus, the more I wanted to pray and follow him as friend rather than just as servant. At the end of a day, the question, "What did I enjoy doing today?" would reveal to me the times I let Jesus' love touch me that day and gradually would help me to work less compulsively and with more joy.

Initiative and Our Image of God

As I healed memories and did little things with joy and love, slowly my image of God changed. God is not a killjoy who is happiest when I am saddest and suffering the cross. In fact, the Jewish Talmud says, "In the world to come, each of us will be called to account for all the good things God put on earth which we refused to enjoy."[6] But unlike the Jewish heritage, my German-Irish heritage tempts me to try to win God's love by hard work, and suffering. St. Teresa of Avila saw this temptation and could shout, "From somber, serious, sullen saints save us, O Lord!" Although Teresa loved to pray over the passion, she said that whenever Jesus appeared to her, he was always risen and smiling with love. The masochist carries the cross; the Christian carries God's love with or without the cross. Jesus saved the world not because he carried the cross but because he experienced and gave us God's love equally while playing with children (Mk 10:13–16) and while carrying the cross. During my thirty-day retreat I welded six crosses and kept for my wall not the final one I did best but the first one I enjoyed most. Because it was my first attempt, it had the most mistakes but reminded me how I was loved with my mistakes and my child-like initiatives. The cross that opens me to receive the most love and to initiate new life is the one Jesus and I want to embrace. Jesus' cross reveals my God who initiates and risks everything to love me and empowers me to risk everything that leads me to give and receive more love.

One of the most healing prayers developing from this play age is praise. Praise opens me to trusting and boasting in God's love. Praise is like a child's prayer—I boast about how my dad is bigger than anyone else's dad. I boast with my hands, voice and whole body that my God is infinitely beyond what I can ask or imagine (Eph 3:20). If I have fear before giving a workshop, I just start to praise God's power to act and my expectations get bigger and bigger. Then I can go into that workshop with a trusting sense of how God is going to move. I can hear God's will in new dreams and initiate the things God is asking me to do without saying, "Well, I don't think that's going to work." Praise is the prayer form that has most freed the child in me that needs to dream and initiate new risks empowered by God's initiative.

For years I looked down on the prayer of praise for three reasons: I thought it degraded God into an egotistical movie star needing adulation, it seemed to be taught as a prayer to get one's own way with God, and it seemed to deny my "negative" emotions. These are all dangers if the person praying has not moved through stage one's trust in God's love and stage two's integration of God's will with one's own deepest will. But as I trust in God's love, I see that praise is not for God's inflated ego but to open me to receive power and love by focusing on God's care rather than just on my problem. Nor is praise to instantly solve problems, as if just praising God for poverty will automatically bring money in the mail. Praise has power not to manipulate God but to open me to my deepest longing for God's will as I proclaim that God is everything for me. As I discover that God's desires are also my deepest desires, my prayer is united to the powerful prayer of Jesus. Nor does praise transform me into a smiling Polyanna out of touch with emotions such as fear and anger. As I trust more in God's love, I can offer praise for all of God's reality including my "negative" emotions which reveal hurts God wants to heal. I praise God not for the problem and its destruction but for how God has alerted me to it and is helping me now and in the future with my cooperation.

Healing the Play Age

God's dreams to heal are infinitely beyond what I can ask or imagine. Judith MacNutt's account of how God healed Sue expands my vision of what God wants to do. At age eighteen, after years of fruitless therapy for her delusions and hallucinations, psychiatrists labeled Sue a "paranoid schizophrenic" destined to spend the rest of her life existing in a mental hospital. Thirty years later Sue was brought to Judith for therapy. After three frustrating, fruitless sessions, Judith suggested she and Sue ask Jesus to show them when Sue's illness began.

Sue began to see herself as three years old, at the time her father suffered a heart attack. Sue would visit her hospitalized, comatose father every day and cling to his hand. Since her mother abused her, Sue's father was the only source of love in Sue's life. Finally one day Sue was told to sit out in the hall while doctors rushed into her father's room. Soon her mother stormed out of the room and dragged Sue down the corridor. Sue said, "I want to say goodby to my daddy." Her mother hit her and screamed, "You will never see your daddy again. He's dead. If I ever see you crying or hear you talk about him again, I'll beat you." So Sue swallowed her tears, anger and loneliness, and returned home with her mother who threw out all her dad's things.

Sue asked Judith, "Do you think this might be the memory that began my illness?" Judith nodded and said, "Sue, can you see yourself again sitting on that chair in the hall?" "Yes." "Do you feel like you are three years old?" "Yes." "Now see if you can see Jesus come down the hall." After a minute, Sue said, "Yes, he is coming down the hall." Then her face lit up and Judith just let her silently be with Jesus for several minutes.

Afterwards, Sue told Judith what had happened. Jesus came down the hospital corridor and said, "Hi. How are you?" Sue answered, "Oh, not so good. They won't let me go in there." Jesus said, "Well, they're not going to stop me. So Jesus took Sue by the hand, led her into the room, woke up her father, and placed Sue in his arms. Sue wept her held-back tears and told her father all the things she had never told him, and reveled in his hugs and kisses. Then Jesus told Sue, "You know, I would like to take your daddy to be with my daddy." Sue asked, "What's your daddy like?" Jesus responded, "He's just like me." Jesus looked at Sue with such love in his eyes that she knew her daddy would really be loved if he were with such a loving father. Like a three-year-old, Sue asked, "Where does your daddy live?" "Not far." "Can I come to visit my daddy?" "No, but someday you can come. I will come to get you myself." "O.K." Then Jesus said, "Why don't you hug your daddy and say goodby to him now?" Sue hugged her daddy and said, "Goodby. I'll see you later." Then Jesus carried her out of the room.

Sue went back to the mental hospital. A few weeks later she called Judith and said, "When I got back to the hospital, they noticed right away something was different. They tested me several times, told me I was perfectly normal, and finally released me!" Sue is still free from all the schizophrenic symptoms she had suffered for over forty years. Sue now prays with women who are depressed or suicidal, because she knows what it is like to be in their painful world and to have Jesus transform it.

A child hurt during this stage of initiative need not wait forty years for healing. Even a small child can use the gift of this stage, imagination, to experience healing, as in the story of Manuelito. Manuelito's mother noticed that since age three Manuelito had been afraid of being left alone in a room, a car, or any other place with a door that might close. He was afraid the door would close and lock, leaving him unable to get out. Yet Manuelito couldn't recall ever being locked in a room. Finally his sister remembered that three years earlier she had been stuck in an elevator with her three-year-old panicking brother. So Manuelito's mother sat down with him and had him draw an elevator with himself inside. Manuelito drew the elevator buttons way above his reach. Then while she prayed, she had him close his eyes, imagine the elevator, feel his panic and then see Jesus standing next to him. He could see it all and experienced Jesus lifting him up to reach the elevator buttons. Jesus told Manuelito, "You are soon going to be big enough to reach the buttons yourself, and you will never again have to worry about getting locked in." All Manuelito's panic evaporated and he drew a tall Jesus in the picture, totally in control. After that prayer, Manuelito had no more fear of elevators, being locked in, etc. A short time later, he was locked alone in the school gym for two hours and had no fear. Manuelito told his mother, "I just closed my eyes and saw Jesus standing next to me. I knew I would be O.K."

How Can Imagination Heal?

The prayer that follows is the "Prayer of Creative Imagination," the prayer that healed Sue and Manuelito. You may have some questions about this type of prayer. Perhaps you wonder how a prayer based on imagination can accomplish anything "real." Yet an experience based on the use of imagination need not be "just imaginary." When St. Joan of Arc was accused by her inquisitors of only imagining her visions, Joan replied, "Of course I imagined them. How else would the Lord speak to me?"

Imagination is our "inner eye," a faculty of our intuitive mind, through which we perceive the emotional and spiritual world, a world just as real as the material one we perceive with our five senses. Jesus uses the inner eye of imagination to help us "see" with him events that have left emotional and spiritual scars, and to help us reinterpret those events in the light of his love. The "Prayer of Creative Imagination" is not a pushbutton means of causing Jesus to do what we imagine. Rather, it is a means of helping ourselves experience how Jesus is already saying and doing the most loving thing at every moment of our lives, past and present.

When Manuelito "saw" himself in the elevator with Jesus, he was able to reinterpret a traumatic experience of helplessness as a loving experience of protection and encouragement. What Manuelito saw was not "just imaginary." Jesus really had been there in that elevator, but Manuelito could not see this until he looked at the event through the inner eye of imagination. What Manuelito experienced is what Jairus, his wife and friends experienced when Jesus told them to see Jairus' daughter as "not dead but asleep." Jesus frequently emphasized how our thoughts and beliefs affect reality, and he wanted the dead girl's loved ones to see her as alive so their hearts could be open to the healing Jesus wanted to do in the girl. (Lk. 8:40–56)

Perhaps you are comfortable with the idea of praying with the imagination, but think others can pray this way better than yourself because you never "see" anything in prayer. Although visual images are usually stressed in this type of prayer, all the senses can be used in imagination. Manuelito not only saw Jesus, but also heard Jesus speak and felt Jesus lift him up to reach the elevator buttons. Each person is unique, and while visual images may come easily to one person, another may more easily imagine sounds, smells, tastes or touch.[7] Feel free to use your imagination in whatever way is most comfortable for you.

Finally, perhaps you cannot remember any painful events from childhood and wonder what to pray for. If you cannot remember a painful event from the play age, you can use an imaginary event like the broken teacup scene which began this chapter. Although such an event may never have happened, as you imagine your own feelings and attitudes, and those of your parents, you will be in touch with real feelings and attitudes that you carry in your heart from real but forgotten events.

The first step of the prayer that follows is to recall a time of being loved and to breathe in that love, since we can face hurt only to the extent that we feel loved. Often it is helpful to have another person pray this prayer with us, as that person's loving presence can be God's way of loving us. Manuelito was able to face the pain of being stuck in the elevator because of his mother's loving presence as she prayed with him. If you get in touch with too much pain as you enter a hurtful memory, then return to the first step or to any other part of the prayer where you felt loved and take in that love in whatever simple way is helpful to you, e.g., breathe it in, hear Jesus repeat a loving word over and over, feel his arm around you, etc. The important thing in this prayer is not the vividness of the images or praying through the whole memory, but rather taking in love wherever you are.

Prayer of Creative Imagination

a. Recall a time when you felt deeply loved. Reexperience the scene, breathing that love into yourself once again.

b. Now recall a time from the play age, especially a time when you were hurt. Reexperience the scene, using all your senses to imagine it. Get in touch with any feelings of hurt. If you cannot recall any memories from this stage, recall the imaginary scene at the beginning of this chapter, in which you broke your mother's best teacup.

c. Let Jesus join you in the scene. Watch what he says and does for you.

d. Breathe in all the ways Jesus is loving you, and breathe out any hurt.

School Age
(Industry vs. Inferiority)

This Year I Will Do Better

I thought, "This year I will do better. . . . Study hard, listen, take good notes, and when he calls on me, I'll give the answer in a loud clear voice, and not just a good answer but a brilliant one. . . .

Then October came and I didn't understand anything. I was scared that he'd call on me and fear made the air around me hot and dry, creating teacher suction, and he drew close to me and said, "Go up and see what you can do," so I stood at the blackboard, looked at the problem, and thought, "God, take this chalk and write the answer. Or make the blackboard fall off and kill me. Please." I wrote a few faint numbers and the smart kids laughed.

[Garrison Keillor, "Leaving Home"]

Can you remember a time between ages six and twelve when you went to school? Imagine climbing the school steps, opening the heavy door, and walking down the hall. Smell the Lysol antiseptic, musty sweeping compound, choking chalk dust, floor wax. Turn into your classroom and sit at your old desk. Do you remember which one? Who sat behind you and in front? Who is the teacher? See the teacher getting ready to ask a question and looking right at you. Are you feeling competent, or inferior and afraid? How do you answer? How do the teacher and other students react? How do you feel?

Perhaps you experienced competence, knowing immediately what the teacher was going to ask and firing back the answer. More likely you experienced not being quite ready to respond, wishing the teacher had called on someone else, or buying more time by asking a question to cover your feeling of inferiority. At this stage, you needed to hear not only "You are good," but also "You are doing well. You are learning well." But for every memory of competence from hearing praise, most people have five memories of feeling inferior from hearing, "That's wrong."

Erikson believes that during the stage of industry (the school age, from six to twelve), children focus especially on feeling competent as they learn well and do well, or on inferiority as they fail. In this as in all the stages, we believe the real task is discovering a new way of giving and receiving love with others. Thus, school is not just a place to acquire competence through knowledge and skills, but rather an opportunity to experience the intimacy of shared learning with peers and teachers.

At this stage teachers have great power to make us feel competent or inferior. In one experiment called "The Self-Fulfilling Prophecy," researchers told elementary teachers, "We are going to test your students to find the spurters, the students who will blossom this year." After the testing they gave each teacher a list of the students who would be spurters. At the end of the year they retested the students and found that in each classroom the five students designated as spurters had advanced as much as three years in one year's time, and their IQ scores had risen 12–36 points. The teachers were ecstatic and asked the researchers to return each year to identify the spurters. The researchers replied something like this: "You really don't need us. We just took five names at random. You thought these five would be spurters so you paid extra attention to them. You had more positive expectation each time you asked them a question and so they answered in a way that would meet your expectations. Every student is shaped by your expectations."[1]

Students too have great power to shape the reactions of not only fellow students but even of teachers. One psychology class decided to program their teacher. As a group they agreed to ignore his lecture until he walked over to the door. When he approached the door, all their heads would go up with rapt attention. He spent the rest of the semester teaching from the doorway, feeling competent as he stood there rather than inferior.

Were You Gifted But Ignored?

Unfortunately our schools make it easier to feel inferior than to feel competent. We generally praise only those few at the top—the A student, the state championship basketball team, the homecoming queen—and tell the others, "Too bad you lost out. Maybe next year you'll be on top." Such competition shows the top person how she is superior but shows everyone else how he is inferior. Social scientists Roger & David Johnson have demonstrated that competition is not the best motivation for learning. They have trained teachers in many school districts in methods which include small cooperative learning groups and no individual grades. In this atmosphere of cooperation, children learn better, feel better about themselves and relate better to others.[2]

Thomas Edison, even after his 2000th attempt at inventing the light bulb, knew the value of continued cooperation. His discouraged assistant complained, "All our work is in vain. We have learned nothing." Edison replied, "We have come a long way and learned a lot. We now know there are 2000 elements we cannot use to make a good lightbulb." When they finally succeeded in making a lightbulb that Edison thought would work, his nervous assistant dropped it. They worked around the clock and made another and then Edison again handed it to his shaking assistant to test. Edison knew it was more important to risk dropping another lightbulb than deny his assistant a chance to regain his sense of competence. Our schools will develop more Thomas Edisons when they teach his attitude toward cooperation and competence rather than only reward the most successful.

Even if we were competent in our own way, we may not have been rewarded. Those competent in art, music and dancing generally do not receive the praise given to those competent in reading, writing and math—the skills stressed in school. Likewise, schools reward thinkers more than feelers. Thinkers value the logical pursuit of truth, whereas feelers place more value on relationships. John-ny's report card praises his A on a math exam, but ignores that he started the semester with one friend and now has four friends. Thus artists and feelers will often feel incompetent during the school years, not because they don't have gifts, but because their gifts are not affirmed in school.

Besides being divided into thinkers and feelers, we are also divided into intuitives and sensates. Intuitive people dream, live in the future, and have considered all the possible questions even before the teacher asks one. They are ready and can respond quickly. In contrast, sensate people live in the present and take in all the data. A sensate is concerned not about the question the teacher is going to write on the blackboard, but that no one has erased the blackboard well and that the chalk is too short. It takes an intuitive person only one second to answer a teacher's question, but even if a sensate knows the answer it takes him three seconds to give it—three times as long. Many teachers won't wait three times as long, but instead label the sensate student as "slow" and therefore will ask another student. When teachers were trained to take three times as long with sensate students, those students blossomed. I.Q. tests also favor the quick intuitive, and research indicates that sensate students score lower, an average of 7.8 points lower for males and 6.7 points for females.[3] Again, we can be hurt not because we don't have gifts, but because we don't have the gifts that school rewards. Both Albert Einstein and Werner von Braun flunked math courses before their gifts were recognized.

Hurts in this stage, especially those which lead us to earn love by working harder, may result in the Type A personality referred to in Chapter Two. The Type A person is not only heart attack prone, but also a compulsive, competitive worker striving to do as much as possible in the least amount of time.[4] Thus, Type A people go through yellow lights, eat fast, do two things at once (e.g., read the newspaper and watch TV), push elevator buttons several times, finish another's sentences, can't delegate work well, and compete with themselves if they are not competing with another. They always think they are in the slowest line and keep shifting to find a faster one. (I am always in the slowest line so I send Dennis and Sheila to stand in the other ticket lines rather than wishing I were there. They always get waited on first and then I join them in that line.) As a perfectionist who receives many rewards for doing well, the Type A person thinks he has to keep doing well to earn love.

While Type A people often succeed (e.g., in school and work) and learn to earn love by trying hard, other less successful people learn not to try at all. We might call them "Type Z." The Type Z person learns (usually in school) that he will fail at whatever he tries, so he tends to say, "Let them do it. I don't want to try anything new because I will probably fail." Both Type A and Type Z need to discover that they are good and their worth doesn't depend on success or failure. They both need G. K. Chesterton's advice that "if something is worth doing at all, it's worth doing poorly."

Industry and Our Image of God

We can also relate to God with the perfectionism of Type A or the sloth of Type Z. We can mistakenly feel God is reacting like a teacher or parent, loving us more if we do well and less if we fail. We go to Mass or do good works to earn God's love rather than as grateful responses to God loving us so much. But God's love doesn't turn on and off like a water faucet. God is a Father whose sun rises on the just and unjust (Mt. 5:45) and a Mother who loves us whether we are competent or incompetent, whether we have worked a full day or an hour (Mt. 20:1–17). God's love doesn't fluctuate, but rather we fluctuate in our capacity to receive God's love. Sunday Mass and good works are not to convince God to love us. Rather, they open us to receive God's everpresent, infinite love and enable us to share it.

While the Type A person is tempted to a Pelagian earning of God's love by trying to work and pray more perfectly, the Type Z person is tempted to dismiss the value of any work or prayer. The Type Z will dismiss her ability to pray, to listen to God in Scripture, to have a personal relationship with God, or to learn more about God. In contrast, the true mystic doesn't rely on her ability to pray well nor does she give up because she can't pray well. The true mystic knows that God's love is an unearned gift and she longs to pray even when she can't.

The gift of prayer that develops in Erikson's fourth stage is contemplation in action prayer. The contemplative in action doesn't meet God in formal prayer and then say "Good-bye" to God as he heads off to work. Rather, as Dag Hammarskjold said, "In our day the road to holiness necessarily passes through the world of action."[5] Thus, the contemplative in action works with God to give and receive love while he works (Rom. 8:28). Thus he lives out Mother Teresa's goal: "Wash a dish not just to get it clean but because you love the person who will eat from it." The true contemplative becomes aware not only of giving love by washing a dish but also of receiving love: the dish and its food become unearned gifts from a loving God who would die for the dishwasher. The Lord won't love him any more or any less even if he breaks the dish or burns the roast.

The contemplative in action loves to work because work is a time of being loved whether there is success or failure.[6]

Jesus teaching in the temple at age twelve models contemplation in action and the ideal of stage four's "competence": a trust in God's competence and letting God use our competence in loving God's people. Jesus knew that he must be about God's important work and that he could do it well, as "all who heard him were amazed at his intelligence and his answers" (Lk. 2:47). Jesus knew that God called him to a special work and felt so loved when doing it that he didn't miss his parents for three days.

Twelve-year-old Jesus teaching in the temple illustrates not only contemplation in action and the task of competence at this stage, but also how such action builds on the previous stages. Jesus' basic trust of his God (Stage 1) led to autonomous separation from doing only his parents' will (Stage 2), to joyfully exploring new dreams such as teaching in the temple (Stage 3), and discovering competence as he industriously undertook this new work (Stage 4). The contemplative in action also finds his work deepens growth in previous stages. To see if I am working compulsively or contemplatively, I can ask: Am I growing in trust (stage 1), hunger to find my deepest desires and thus God's will (stage 2), zeal to take new initiatives even after failure (stage 3)? Do I enjoy what I am doing (Stage 4), or am I just eager to get it done?

Positive and Negative Memories in the Stage of Industry

When I (Sheila) think about my negative memories from this stage, the effect of my mother's illness stands out (mentioned in Chapter 2). Because of her illness she behaved in inappropriate ways in public that resulted in social ostracism. For example, when I would accompany her to the drugstore in our neighborhood, she would suddenly begin to scream hysterically at me or at the druggist, while several of the neighborhood children and their parents watched. This led to our family developing a negative reputation in the community. I always dreaded revealing my last name when meeting a new person, because I feared they might have heard of my mother and might ridicule me. Constant feelings of shame and embarrassment made me withdraw and thus I could not relate to other children.

Perhaps the most important task in this stage of the school age is not learning to do things well, but learning to do things well with others. In school I felt so much fear of ridicule, shame and embarrassment that I could barely pay attention to anything else. The teacher would ask me a question, and all I could think of was that I felt strange and alone.

My teachers told me I was very bright and competent, and objectively I did well, even skipping fourth grade. But I always felt my inner self was paralyzed and that I was not able to learn as deeply as I could if I were free. I felt withdrawn from even the physical objects of learning, such as the pencils and the books. Deep within I yearned to engage fully with the objects of learning, just as I yearned to engage fully with the other children. Years later, as an adult, I visited an empty Montessori classroom, filled with beautiful objects beckoning children into the world of learning. I began to feel waves of grief, and cried hard for a long time. I realized that I was grieving for all the crayons and the books that I could relate to only from a distance as a child.

My other painful memory from the school age is that

parts of me could not relate to school even at a distance. School emphasized certain skills, especially verbal and mathematical skills—things which I could do well. But other skills I had, such as a deep spiritual sensitivity, were not valued. This sensitivity to God and to the goodness in all created things became a secret inside of me, something I was sure no one at school would understand. While in school I did not feel loved, either because I was too withdrawn to take in the affirmation that was there, or because certain gifts were not affirmed. Thus I was not really free to learn.

What Were the Positive Memories?

My positive memories are of times at my grandparents' home, when I did feel loved and when I was really free to learn. My mother's parents were healthy, loving people and highly respected in their Jewish community. They were always concerned about me, as they knew my mother was not able to care for a child. They invited me into their home as often as possible, and I frequently visited them on weekends and spent many childhood summers at their vacation beach home. During these visits, especially the long summer ones, I changed dramatically. A week or two after I arrived at the beach, I would emerge from my withdrawal and begin to enjoy myself with the other children whose families owned summer homes nearby. By the end of the summer I would be one of the most popular children, amazed at the way the others liked me and followed me as I thought up ways to have fun.

In this environment of love and social acceptance, I joyfully learned everything I was taught. For example, my grandmother taught me how to cook. She would move her big kitchen stool next to the stove for me. As I sat on the stool and watched, she explained everything she did and then let me try it myself. Ever since then, I have instinctively known how to cook anything and make it really good. (Matt and Dennis are Chinese food *addicts* and about five years ago we got a wok and some Chinese cookbooks. We are now better than all known Chinese restaurants . . . or at least our friends think so!) My grandmother also taught me sewing, knitting and crocheting. I learned so well that at six years old I could make sweaters. Today I have extremely good fine motor coordination and can make almost anything with my hands. Not only my mind and my muscles learned better in the atmosphere of love I felt with my grandmother, but I also learned from her a sensitivity to all of life. She would take me for long walks on the beach, and she kept me beside her as she worked in her garden. I learned from her a loving sensitivity to nature, so that now I can love any plant into life. Sometimes I even think I can hear my alfalfa sprouts growing.

Not only did my grandparents provide a loving atmosphere for learning, but they also provided a home for the spiritual side of me. As Jewish immigrants my grandparents continued to observe their faith in America. I often watched my grandfather get ready to go to the synagogue. He would put on his yarmulke (skullcap) and prayer shawl, and pick up his Hebrew Bible. As I watched him, I would feel a wave of something ancient and deep go through me. I sensed that I stood at the end of generations of ancestors who had done the same as my grandfather. I felt myself a part of a profound spiritual tradition where there was a home for all the secret questions and intuitions in my own heart. This tradition was like a mysterious presence that seemed to fill even the corners of my grandparents' house, so that I breathed it into myself just by being there. Although I did not consciously know Jesus until adulthood, I think my capacity to relate to him in contemplative prayer first developed as I breathed in the mysterious presence that lived in the corners of my grandparents' house.

Love Brings Out the Most Hidden Gift

Not only I but even the most handicapped person can develop hidden gifts in an atmosphere of love. One dramatic example of this is Leslie Lemke.[7] Leslie was born in 1952, with cerebral palsy and severe mental retardation. His eyes became infected and had to be removed, leaving him blind. Leslie's parents abandoned him in the hospital when he was six months old. The hospital personnel expected him to die. They asked foster parents May and Joe Lemke if they would take Leslie home and care for him until he died. The Lemke's agreed to take Leslie home, but said, "No one comes to our house to die!"

May and Joe kept Leslie alive. But for nine years he never responded to them in any way and never even moved a muscle on his own. May and Joe continued to love Leslie, holding him, talking to him and praying for him. At nine years old, he moved one hand for the first time. After that, Leslie gradually learned to walk by pulling himself along the back fence. But he was still so uncoordinated that he could not even feed himself. When Leslie was twelve, May and Joe began to pray, "Lord, everyone has a special gift. Give Leslie a special gift too." Soon after that, they noticed that when Leslie heard music, he would move his fingers as if trying to keep time with it. Since he seemed to like music, they decided to buy a piano. May would hold Leslie next to her on the piano bench with one hand and play simple tunes with the other. As she sang, she held her cheek next to Leslie's, hoping he might somehow learn that his mouth could make sounds.

One night when Leslie was sixteen, the Lemkes had been watching "Liberace" on television. After everyone had gone to bed, May woke up and heard music. She thought perhaps someone had left the television on. When May went downstairs to check, she saw Leslie at the piano. He was playing Tschaikovsky's First Piano Concerto (theme song for "Liberace") and playing it perfectly. His fingers raced over the keys as gracefully as the most skilled pianist. Yet when he finished, he could not even sit up on the piano bench by himself. May and Joe soon learned that Leslie could play any song he heard after hearing it only once. Leslie had still never spoken a word, but when he was nineteen he suddenly began singing . . . a Frank Sinatra song! Now Leslie could sing as well as play any song, after hearing it only once. Leslie began to give benefit concerts (for the "less fortunate"), and his parents traveled with him. May would speak to audiences about the power of love and prayer to bring forth hidden gifts in even the most handicapped person. When asked by a psychiatrist how she could explain Leslie's remarkable gift for music, May said, "I always treated him like a normal person . . . like a person who had potential."

Healing the School Age

Although most are not as severely handicapped as Leslie, all of us probably have some part of us that feels handicapped. Any hurt during this stage can damage our sense of competence and leave us feeling handicapped in some area.

Fortunately, we can pray with a school age child for healing of even the most traumatic hurts. For example, our friend Eileen (a therapist) prayed with six-year-old Sara, whose teenage cousin sexually abused her. Sara came with her mother and her favorite doll. First Eileen asked Sara to share what had happened. Sara pointed on her doll to the parts of the body where her cousin had touched her and said, "My doll is angry about being touched like that." Eileen affirmed Sara's anger, explained to her the difference between "good touch" and "bad touch," and told Sara it was O.K. to refuse "bad touch." Then Eileen asked Sara to hold hands with her mother and her doll, and to see Jesus with her during the abuse. Sara saw Jesus standing on her cousin's shoulders and telling him in a firm voice, "I want you to go and tell your parents right now." Then Sara told Jesus she felt stupid because she had been afraid to tell her cousin to stop touching her. Jesus told Sara she wasn't stupid and that he was proud of her, especially for telling her mother. Finally Jesus hugged Sara, and Sara hugged Jesus back.

In this prayer, Jesus healed Sara of emotional damage typical of sexual abuse victims: feelings of helplessness (by speaking to Sara's cousin in a firm voice), shame and guilt (by telling Sara she wasn't stupid for being afraid to stop her cousin, and by affirming her for "telling on" her cousin), and fear of touch (by hugging her with "good touch"). This healing prayer may have saved Sara from many years, perhaps even a lifetime, of being traumatized by her experience of sexual abuse.

If during our school years we did not have someone like Eileen to pray with us for our hurts, we can still pray for healing now. For instance, I have noticed in many people a common school age hurt, fear of writing. When we give a retreat and ask participants to fill out evaluations, many people will ask if they are "doing it right." There is no *right* way to fill out an evaluation! Writing seems to represent many of the ways people felt incompetent in school, as if they never "did it right." One such person was Mary. I met Mary when she attended one of our *Prayer Course for Healing Life's Hurts* groups (see Appendix C). During the first session, when I introduced the daily "Writing Prayer," Mary became very upset. She said, "I can't write." When I asked Mary why she couldn't write, she told me the following story.

In second grade, Mary attended a Christian school in which her father was the principal. Thus Mary always felt that whatever she did reflected on her father. One day, Mary's religion teacher asked the students to write "Spirit." Instead, Mary wrote "Sprite." The teacher called Mary up to the front of the classroom and ridiculed her before the whole class. Mary, deeply humiliated, feared her mistake would embarrass her father. From then on, Mary was afraid to write because she feared making mistakes and further embarrassing her father. In Mary's mind, if teachers and her father would be displeased, then God too certainly would be displeased. As Mary saw her father, teachers, God and everyone else as demanding perfection, Mary demanded perfection of herself.

I asked Mary if she would be willing to write to Jesus about her very fear of writing. Although frightened, Mary agreed to try. Over the next few weeks, Mary began to tell Jesus all her fears about writing. Mary was so frightened of making mistakes that her very fear caused her to make spelling and grammatical mistakes. But she tried to focus on sharing her heart with Jesus rather than on a perfect composition. After weeks of hearing Jesus' loving responses to her, Mary shared her deepest fear about writing, her second grade hurt. Jesus responded,

"Mary, I understand the hatred and anger you feel. I too am angry at the destruction you have experienced. No child should be ridiculed as you were. Your teacher treated you so cruelly only because she was a very wounded person and had been treated cruelly herself. But I am not like your teacher, and I will love you no matter how many mistakes you make."

Because Jesus shared Mary's anger, Mary felt loved and understood by Jesus. She was now ready to forgive her teacher.

As Mary forgave her teacher, her fear of writing began to disappear. As she became less frightened, she actually made fewer mistakes and felt more competent at writing. But the greatest healing Mary experienced was learning that God is not a perfectionist. Mary learned that God loves her unconditionally, whether or not she makes mistakes.

The following is the prayer that healed Mary.

Writing Prayer

a. Get in touch with a memory from between the ages of six and twelve, especially a hurtful memory of a time when you felt incompetent. You might imagine entering your old classroom, as suggested at the beginning of this chapter. Ask yourself when you felt stupid and unable to do things right. Rather than begin by recalling a school age memory, you might prefer to get in touch with a time in your present life when you feel incompetent, and then see if Jesus shows you when it began.

b. Briefly share your feelings with Jesus in writing. You might begin with "Dear Jesus," and then write as if you were writing a love letter to your best friend, sharing what you feel most deeply. Don't worry about having the "right" words, but only try to share your heart.

For example, Mary might have written something like this:

> "Dear Jesus, I hate that teacher for laughing at me! How could she be so cruel. I can't forget the sound of her laughter. Every time I try to write I hear it again and I feel so stupid."

c. Now get in touch with Jesus' response to you, as he is already speaking to you within. You might do this by asking what are the most loving words that you want him to say to you in response, or perhaps by imagining that what you have just written is a note to you from the person you love most, and you want to respond to that person in the most loving possible words.

d. Write Jesus' response. Perhaps it will be just one word or one sentence. You can be sure that anything you write which helps you to know more clearly that you are loved is not just your own thoughts or imagination but is really what Jesus wants to say to you.

You may wish to recall what Mary wrote as Jesus' response:

> "Dear Mary, I understand the hatred and anger you feel. . . . But I am not like your teacher, and I will love you no matter how many mistakes you make."

Chapter 5:

Adolescence
(Identity vs. Identity Confusion)

The Golden Eagle

A man found an eagle's egg and put it in the nest of a backyard hen. The eaglet hatched with the brood of chicks and grew up with them.

All his life the eagle did what the backyard chickens did, thinking he was a backyard chicken. He scratched the earth for worms and insects. He clucked and cackled. And he would thrash his wings and fly a few feet into the air.

Years passed and the eagle grew very old. One day he saw a magnificent bird far above him in the cloudless sky. It glided in graceful majesty among the powerful wind currents, with scarcely a beat of its strong golden wings.

The old eagle looked up in awe. "Who's that?" he asked.

"That's the eagle, the king of the birds," said his neighbor. "He belongs to the sky. We belong to the earth—we're chickens."

So the eagle lived and died a chicken, for that's what he thought he was.

[Anthony DeMello, *The Song of the Bird*]

119

If you can remember getting ready for your senior prom, you will probably understand what Erikson means by the stage of identity. The senior prom marks the end to a secure existence and marks the beginning of the realization that very soon I'm going to have to leave home and be on my own. Thus, in this stage the adolescent (age 12–18) tries to make the transition from childhood to adulthood. During this transition, the adolescent vacillates between being very much of a child (e.g., being festive and dancing) and being very much of an adult (strutting around in a tuxedo or a formal dress). And when the music stops, the adolescent frequently tries to escape and find a mirror, hoping there's a better way to put himself together. Whether in front of the mirror or elsewhere, the adolescent scrutinizes each new acne blemish and asks the identity questions: Who am I? What am I doing here? What am I going to be?

To help you experience this stage, you may wish to recall a time when you were between twelve and eighteen years old and see how you would have answered these identity questions. Perhaps try and remember your senior prom or another time on a date. Can you remember what you wore and what your date wore that evening?

What did your date think about you? How would your date describe you in a sentence? Were you seen as a macho man or as a cute cheerleader?

How would you describe yourself? Did you want your date to meet your parents or were you ashamed of them? What were your sexual values? Were you one who was known to "go all the way" or "a prude"? Were you happy or sad when the evening was over?

Perhaps many of you can remember, as I can, the senior prom. When prom time came, I (Dennis) had never invited a girl on a date. That was because whenever I looked in the mirror all I usually saw was a short, uncoordinated kid with acne all over his face. But luckily the girls' school had their prom first, and one of the girls there, Kathy, had never gone on a date either. So when it came time for Kathy's senior prom she called me up. She said, "Dennis, would you like to go to my senior prom?" "Sure," I said because I thought, "If I go to hers, I'll find out what these things are like and when mine comes up I'll be all set."

So, I went to her senior prom. I endured it. Then when it came time for my prom, I called Kathy. "Kathy, how would you like to go to my senior prom?" And Kathy said, "Oh, I had such a delightful evening with you." As she began describing what a wonderful time she had with me, I wondered if we really had been at the same event. "Dennis, I'd love to go to your senior prom. But first of all, I have to ask my mother." Although she put down the phone, I could hear her say, "Mom, can I go to Dennis' senior prom?" I think her mother was taken by surprise, but pleased that someone had finally invited Kathy on a date. I heard her mother say, "That sounds great." When Kathy came back to the phone, she said, "Dennis, my mother said I have to babysit. I can't go to your senior prom."

Although I was disappointed at Kathy's response, I wasn't very surprised. I didn't like myself and I didn't think anybody else liked me either. Much of my self-hatred came from being a very scrupulous person, or what Erikson describes as the "autocracy of conscience."[1] This means I defined myself by authorities' values (e.g. teachers, parents, and church leaders), and I became who they said I was. As Erikson describes it, "many a youth, finding that the authorities expect him to be 'a bum' or 'a queer' or 'off the beam' perversely obliges by becoming just that."[2]

In my case, I took on the attitude of many of my pastors and teachers that "God sees sexuality as bad, and you're bad because you can't live up to what God expects." I can remember, for instance, going on a two-week trip. On the first day we stopped at a gas station which had a calendar with Marilyn Monroe in a skimpy swim suit. After staring at the picture, I became frightened that I had committed a mortal sin. Here I was on this trip, spending two weeks in mortal sin and hoping not to have a car accident, lest I die and my soul go immediately to hell. I was always worried about saving my soul. Later, my belief that priests had the best chance of saving their souls was one of the reasons I joined the Jesuits.

Though much of my identity crisis happened because I unquestioningly took on the values of teachers and church authorities, for another adolescent the crisis might take the form of stomping out of church and questioning all the values of authorities. Thinking that everyone else is "old-fashioned," some teens cast away all their family's values and have no anchor. In this stage of "low tolerance," adolescents are ashamed of their parents and find a way to rebel, such as running away, quitting church or even committing suicide.

Frequently, as they rebel against their parents, they will rebel against their parents' God. This may create a faith crisis. Although other circumstances, such as a sudden tragedy, can trigger a faith crisis even in a healthy family. such a crisis happens less often if the parents have a healthy image of God and a healthy relationship with the adolescent. When either of these is lacking, the adolescent frequently feels distant from God in the ways she feels distant from her parents. Thus, an adolescent may rebel against a God who, like her parents, always criticizes and never hugs, loves more when she succeeds, or, like her absent father, can't be counted on. Religious educators have discovered that close bonding with parents is a more important foundation for faith than religious education.[3] Thus, one high school teacher grew so frustrated when trying to teach religion to rebelling teenagers that he now begins the year with these questions: When do I feel closer to my parents? To God? When do I feel more distant from my parents? From God? What did I learn from these questions?

Thus, a faith crisis is often necessary in order to discard the parents' image of God and find one's own. Such a crisis often causes much conflict between parents and adolescents but can be healthy because now the adolescent can commit himself to a God who acts differently from his fallible parents and who loves more than his parents ever imagined.

Not only faith crises but also other conflicts creating crises are often necessary in order for an adolescent to leave home and form her own values. Thus, if for a parent cleanliness or saving money is next to godliness, then Sandy's patched jeans or spending sprees can be healthy signs of Sandy forming her own identity. That is perhaps why Anna Freud wrote that in any other time of life such conflict-creating behavior would be neurotic, bordering on psychosis. But for an adolescent, conflict is normal.

Unless these conflicts are worked out in adolescence, Erikson cautions that even adults can continue to make decisions solely on the basis of what an authority says (autocracy of conscience) or solely in reaction to that authority's "old-fashioned values." Erikson gives as a specific example the question of family size. A couple might slavishly follow their parents' example of having as many children as possible (the autocracy of conscience), or on the other hand, might rebel by having no children at all. But with a healthy identity, the couple deciding about family size can ask, "How can we best use our life-giving power for future generations?"[4]

On the basis of my adolescent prom experience, Erikson could have been talking to me as he described some of the crises that block a healthy identity. "It will be difficult to be tolerant if deep down you are not quite sure . . . that you will ever grow together again and be attractive, that you will be able to master your drives, that you really know who you are."[5] Hating myself, I was unable to be "tolerant" and thus could not choose a healthy identity. With a healthy identity, I would have been able to continually choose (from among all the possibilities presented by parents, teachers, church authorities etc . . .) healthy ways of living that would have defined my personality and hopefully given meaning to myself and others.

How Do I Find Identity?

I tried a lot of possibilities in my search to find a way of living that would give meaning to myself and others. First I tried grades and graduated at the top of my class. Then I tried money and had a bigger bank account than anyone my age. Finally, I entered the seminary and so supposedly resolved what Erikson, rightly or wrongly, suggests is the primary cause of disturbance in adolescents: "the inability to settle on an occupational identity."[6] I tried lots of ways to say "This is who I am." I am what I know, the money I save, the job I do. But I still hated myself and hated life.

The breakthrough came when I was eighteen and made a general confession of all the sins in my life. I had eight pages, single-spaced, of all the things I hated about myself. After I finished my list, the priest, now probably totally exhausted, came over and hugged me. It was the first time a priest had hugged me. Since I judged so many of the sins to be serious, I had expected the usual sermon about how I had disappointed God and needed to make up my mind to try harder or I would ultimately suffer the painful consequences of hell. But in that hug, I met a God who loved the worst part of myself. I can remember going back to my room, crying and feeling like someone who could love much because he had been forgiven much. My identity was given to me at that time, as brother—one who is a brother to all and who can love much because he is forgiven much. That same identity is still with me. Perhaps you may wish to pray the following prayer in order to experience with me a healthy identity built on being able to love much because you are forgiven much.

Prodigal Prayer

You may wish to pray this prayer alone or with another.

a. Ask Jesus to reveal to you the prodigal part of yourself, the part you are most ashamed of.

b. Read Luke 15:11–32 and decide whether you want to be the father or the prodigal. If you are the father, without using words welcome home the prodigal. (If you are alone, do this in your imagination and perhaps with gestures. If you are with another, express yourself nonverbally. If you are a woman, you may wish to be God the Mother.) If you are the prodigal, soak in the love of the Father as he welcomes you home.

c. Reverse roles.

Positive and Negative Memories in the Stage of Identity

Among the areas which Erikson sees as especially important during adolescence are sexual development, belonging to a peer group, and forming one's own moral values. I (Sheila) remember how an experience of sexual abuse hurt me in the first two of these areas, and challenged me in the third.

A man who lived in our neighborhood sexually abused me just before I entered adolescence. This experience affected me profoundly because I never told anyone about it until many years later and so was entirely alone with its traumatic effects.[7] Also, it reinforced wounds from hurts in earlier stages caused by my family situation (see Chapters 2 and 4). At any stage of development, an unhealed hurt will not only affect us at that stage but will also weaken us in all the future stages as well. Thus, I had few emotional reserves to help me with the devastating effects of sexual abuse.

Sexual abuse such as I experienced is one of the most common hurts which participants on our retreats bring for healing. Current research confirms what we find in retreats. In San Francisco, one of the most extensive studies of sexual abuse found that 38% of women have an experience of physical sexual abuse by the age of 18, and for three-fourths of them the abuse occurs by the age of 13.[8] Not only women, but also men experience sexual abuse. The San Francisco study found that 10% of men experience physical sexual abuse by the age of 18. A study in Detroit suggests that the incidence for boys may be as high as for girls, but that boys may be more reluctant to admit sexual victimization. After a program of educating Detroit schoolchildren to report incidents of sexual abuse, the ratio of boys to girls reporting incidents rose from 1:6 to 1:1.[9] Sexual abuse, with all its devastating effects, is very common.

The effects of sexual abuse vary with each person. Some become promiscuous; the incidence of childhood sexual abuse among prostitutes is 90% according to one study,[10] and 50% among women who have multiple abortions.[11] Some become sexual abusers themselves, as in the case of Linda (see Introduction) and the Connecticut Department of Corrections study which found that 81% of violent sexual offenders had themselves been sexually abused as children.[12] Others, like myself, respond to sexual abuse by withdrawing.

I withdrew entirely from relationships with boys and later young men. I did not experience this as a conscious choice, but rather as a total inability to relate to males. Whenever I was in the presence of a male, I felt emotionally and physically paralyzed, unable to move or speak normally. I felt as if I had a knot of iron in the center of my abdomen, with wires extending to my hands, feet and vocal cords which became taut with fear. To avoid being noticed, I made myself as unattractive as possible, dressing in shapeless clothes and holding myself in a bent over posture.[13] When I look at pictures of myself taken during that time, I see a terrified person.

These pictures represented well my inner state. I felt terrified. I also felt ugly and full of a nameless guilt, as if my very existence as a woman was bad. This pervasive guilt, a symptom I have found in every sexual abuse case shared with me, researchers confirm as virtually universal.[14] No matter how obviously coerced, sexual abuse victims usually assume they caused the abuse. They frequently then transfer this self-blame to other life situations, habitually assuming they are wrong and others are right. In addition to terror and guilt, I also felt grief. As I moved through adolescence and watched other girls become women, I grieved for the loss of the woman I was supposed to be. I felt as if my feminine identity had been taken from me and would never be restored. Unable to even date, I was stuck in the pre-adolescent stage when the abuse had taken place.

It was not until age eighteen that I connected my inability to relate to boys with my childhood experience of sexual abuse; I had so repressed this memory that it had never occurred to me as the root of my teenage difficulties. When I realized the connection, I sought healing through counseling. In our ministry, we frequently recommend counseling. But counseling, when given by a mature, loving person willing to become emotionally involved with the client (in appropriate ways), has greater power to heal when combined with prayer. Unfortunately, the counseling I received was not combined with prayer, and was given by a person trained to maintain "clinical distance." Such counseling brought me insight, but not healing.[15]

Healing Memories through the Prayer of Creative Imagination

When I did find healing, it came through loving community and inner healing prayer. When others, especially loving couples, prayed with me, we often prayed the "Prayer of Creative Imagination" (see Chapter 3). In this prayer, I got in touch with a painful memory, and entered that scene in my imagination. I invited Jesus to join me there, and then watched what he said and did. This prayer is based on Jesus' power to heal painful memories by filling them with his love. Healing of memories does not mean we no longer remember the painful event, but rather that we no longer experience the pain or other crippling aftereffects.

As loving friends prayed the "Prayer of Creative Imagination" with me, they invited me to return in my imagination to the scene of sexual abuse and invite Jesus to join me there. We prayed this way many times, over a period of several months, which is often necessary in praying for a deep hurt. In the prayer experience I recall best, Jesus entered the scene and immediately intervened to stop the abuse. He made it clear to me that he did not like what was happening and was angry about my being hurt. Then Jesus picked me up, held me and comforted me until my fear was gone. I became aware of Mary's presence in the room, and Jesus carried me over to Mary. As I rested in Mary's arms and watched Jesus, he went over to the man who abused me and placed his arm around the man's shoulder. Jesus showed me this man had hurt me only because he was so deeply hurt himself.

In this prayer, Jesus did several things for me that were healing. First, he let me know he was with me in the experience of abuse. This was healing because much of the destructive power of sexual abuse is its quality of hiddenness, leaving the victim feeling alone with a dark and terrible secret. Sharing the experience with those who prayed with me and then having Jesus actually join me in the memory helped remove this dark and secretive quality. Secondly, Jesus intervened to protect me and he let me know he was angry on my behalf. This was healing because victims of sexual abuse feel helpless to protect themselves, and tend to blame themselves rather than feel righteous anger at the abuser. Jesus conveyed to me that *he* would protect me and that, since he was angry on my behalf, I had every right to be angry too.

Then Jesus held me and comforted me until I was no longer afraid. At this point, Jesus was filling in the love I had needed at that time. It is significant that Jesus loved me by holding me, thus replacing an experience of "bad touch" with one of "good touch" and helping to restore my trust of touch as basically good. The way in which Jesus then gave me to Mary was healing because I needed the love of a motherly woman as well as that of a man. Sexually abused girls often feel distant from their mother, feeling shame that they have disgraced womanhood and anger that their mother did not protect them. Finally, Jesus gave me his understanding and compassion for the man who abused me, which helped me to forgive that man. Perhaps one reason the love of Jesus and Mary was so tangible for me in these prayers was that the love of those praying with me, especially couples, was so tangible. With deep hurts, we need to pray with friends who incarnate God's love.

Absorbing Health from Healthy Friends

As I saw how much it helped me to pray with the presence of a loving couple, I began to seek out the presence of loving couples in the rest of my life. I stayed in the presence of such people as much as possible, quietly absorbing their quality of wholesome love for each other. I also avoided individuals or couples who seemed to have disturbances in their sexuality, since I noticed that I felt more frightened and less healed in their presence. Moreover, I had previously received prayer from people with major hurts in their sexuality who only added to the hurt I had already experienced. I needed a human incarnation of healthy sexuality along with the healing power of prayer.[16]

Knowing that I always felt better when I was in the presence of couples who loved each other in a healthy way, I decided when praying alone to ask for the presence of Joseph and Mary, who were the healthiest couple that ever lived. So, I began asking Jesus to take me home with him and share with me his experience of growing up in the atmosphere of healthy love between a man and a woman. I would see myself entering Jesus' birthplace in Bethlehem or his home in Nazareth and hear his family greet me. Then I would breathe in the atmosphere of their love for one another, and breathe out any feelings of fear or darkness. Gradually I began to take in Mary's healthy feminine identity and feel that I deserved to be treated as lovingly and trustworthily as Joseph treated her. I began to breathe in Joseph's trustworthy love and know that other men could be equally trustworthy.

After several months of prayer and of being in the presence of healthy relationships, all my symptoms of sexual abuse disappeared. I no longer felt frightened, frozen, guilty or full of grief. During one prayer time, the "iron knot" in my abdomen seemed to dissolve, and I never felt it again. I began to dress attractively and stand up straighter. People who had not seen me for several months told me I seemed like a different person. And that is how I felt.

Gifts Coming from Hurts

When I look back on this experience, what I see now are the gifts that have come from it. First, I see how it gifted me in forming religious and moral values. Although it was very painful for me during adolescence to be outside the world of dating, the stance of an outsider helped me to see the negative side of that world. I saw how dating could be sexually abusive in its own way, whenever it was based on treating people as sexual objects. Such attitudes are pervasive in our culture, and my experience was only an extreme form of the sexual abuse we all experience every day as we pass billboards, watch television commercials, etc. in which we are encouraged to treat people as sexual objects.

Since I knew only too well how destructive it is to be treated as a sexual object, I concluded even as a young teenager that being a sexual object was not a good basis for relationship between men and women. I came to believe that the communion of persons in friendship was a better basis for relationship, and that in marriage physical sexuality could be a joyful expression of such friendship. And so I began to pray for the gift of being a good friend to men. I have several close male friends now, and when I think of them and especially of Matt and Dennis and the way our ministry is based on our friendship, I believe God has answered my prayer.[17]

Another gift that has come from my experience of sexual abuse is an ability to pray with others who have been abused. I can pray with them because I understand the suffering they feel now and because I have hope for them. Most victims of sexual abuse believe, as I did, that they have been damaged beyond healing. But I know now that sexual abuse can be healed because I know how I have been healed.

Images of Ourselves and Images of God

Sexual abuse can happen in many ways. It includes any way we are not encouraged to develop both the masculine and feminine sides of our personality and of our image of God. In our culture, the feminine dimension of reality is often abused or overlooked because we are biased in favor of masculine ways of perceiving creation, human beings and God.[18] Although Erikson has been accused of sharing this male bias, he does recognize that during adolescence men and women often go about identity formation in different ways.

These differences in identity formation may originate in infancy, where the primary nurturing person is usually the mother. As children, girls experience their gender identity as continuous with or connected to that of their mothers. But boys, in order to define their gender identity as masculine, must begin to see themselves as different or separate from their mothers. Thus male identity tends to be defined through separation, while female identity tends to be defined through connectedness.[19]

Differences in identity formation may arise not only from relationships with the mother but also from differences in body structure. While the male experiences his penis as an instrument for penetration and exploration of a mystery which is essentially external to himself, the female experiences her womb as an internal center of mystery, capable of receiving and nurturing life. During a research study in which 300 school-age children were asked to construct a scene using toys and blocks, Erikson noticed that the 150 boys in the study constructed scenes which consistently differed from the scenes constructed by the 150 girls, in ways that paralleled differences in body structure. The boys tended to build high towers and

houses with protrusions and to describe scenes f
tivity and danger, while the girls tended to build low en-
closures with developed interiors, and to describe peaceful
scenes. Thus, the boys' scenes emphasized outer space,
while the girls' scenes emphasized inner space.[20]

Women Value Connectedness, Men Value Autonomy

Carol Gilligan's *In a Different Voice* confirms Erikson's
observations that men and women approach life differently. Gilligan describes how men tend to make moral
choices based on individual rights, while women tend to
make choices based on maintaining a network of relationships.[21] Erikson, Gilligan and others see women as emphasizing connectedness, relationship, cooperation,
receptivity and "inner space," while men emphasize separation, autonomy, competition, intrusion and "outer
space." This is a generalization, since individuals vary
greatly and since, according to Jung, each of us has a sub-
ordinate sexual identity that complements our dominant
sexual identity. Thus women have a masculine side (or
"animus") and men have a feminine side (or "anima").

Although the idea of differences between men and
women is a generalization, such differences permeate our
values and perceptions of reality in areas as diverse as education, psychology, and religion. Even in scientific research, with its emphasis on cold observable data, women
observe differently and reach different conclusions from
men. For example, most genetic research has been done by
male scientists. They have seen DNA as controlling the
cell, while being itself free of outside influences—i.e., autonomous in its activity. Recently, however, women scientists have found that DNA is much more dependent on

other aspects of cellular life than previously supposed—i.e., connected in its activity.[22]

Women also differ from men in their experience of the educational system that prepares them to do scientific research. Matina Horner gives the example of two medical school students in the same class, John and Anne, each of whom has the chance to graduate as the top-ranked student. For Anne, anticipation of success, especially at John's expense, can cause "success anxiety." "Success anxiety" is triggered by a woman's fear of losing her femininity and is frequently present when her success comes at the expense of another's failure. Anne, whose identity is based on connectedness and relationship, believes that "something is rotten where success is perceived as better grades than everyone else." However, if John graduated first in his medical school class, he would find himself affirmed in his male identity. Achievement in a competitive situation separates John from the others and confirms him in the autonomy upon which his male identity is based.[23]

Women, therefore, base their identity more upon relationship with others and tend to know themselves as they are known, while men tend to base their identity more upon autonomous individuality. Although Erikson recognizes this difference in identity formation, he is criticized for not taking it into consideration in his developmental chart. For example, in Erikson's stages, identity precedes intimacy. This may be correct for men, who emphasize separation in identity formation. But for women, who come to know themselves through connectedness with others, the identity stage may not precede but rather be continuous with the intimacy stage.

Erikson's entire system emphasizes steps toward autonomy and independence, thus implying that separation itself is the model and measure of maturity. Much contemporary psychology shares this emphasis. Thus men, who may have developed one dimension of human maturity, the capacity to be a separate self, are often seen as the ideal. Meanwhile women, who may have developed the overlooked dimension of human maturity, the capacity for connectedness, may be seen as dependent and immature.[24]

Male and Female Views of God

Not only is psychology affected by a male bias, but also religion. Many assumptions of spirituality are based upon male experience. For example, men who have been raised to compete with and dominate others may understandably perceive sin as pride. This male view of sin as pride has become central to Christian spirituality; the remedy is seen as "dying to self." But, "for a woman sin is not pride, the exaltation of self, but a refusal to claim the self God has given."[25] Thus, for a woman, whose growing edge is to assert herself, a male-biased spirituality with its prescription of "dying to self" may simply deepen her bondage to sin rather than heal it. For both men and women, the truth behind the idea of "dying to self" is our need to find our true self rather than live from a false self based upon feelings of either inadequacy or pride.

Not only our spirituality but also its foundation, our image of God, is affected by a male bias. Erikson and James Nelson suggest that the female emphasis upon inner space and the male emphasis upon outer space is reflected in a correspondingly different emphasis in our image of God: men tend to emphasize a transcendent God who lives out beyond us, and women tend to emphasize an immanent God who lives within us.[26] Yet our theology emphasizes God's transcendence, and when our language about God uses male terms exclusively such as "He" and "Father," we are reinforcing this masculine emphasis upon God's transcendence at the expense of God's immanence, and leaving women to wonder in whose image *they* are made.

For example, Joann Conn observes among her women students that those who " 'don't mind that God is pictured only as a man or that we aren't allowed to do the same things men do in the Church' " are constricted in their personal development, whereas those who are developing in their identity experience a strain in their relationship with God if their God image has not included femininity. Thus, if a woman does not see a continuity between her developing identity—her nature as a mature woman—and the nature of God, she will either abandon her own deepest identity or abandon (or at least revise) her belief in God.[27] One woman who struggled to retain her belief in God in the face of her child's death wrote,

> It is with God-the-Mother alone that some of us have had to share the death of a child, so poignantly captured in Ethel Florence Richardson's words of a mother at her child's death bed who weeps, 'They say He knows all, but never, never can He have known what it means to be a mother.'[28]

Since we become like the God we adore, and since masculine language about God perpetuates a masculine image of God, such language perpetuates the male bias throughout our culture and encourages us to further devalue women.[29] In contrast to our culture, for example, there is little or no rape in cultures which have a feminine image of God and where women take an active role in religious ritual.[30] Men who have a feminine image of God not only tend to have better relationships with women, but also are among those most committed to social concerns and most spiritually mature.[31] Genesis assures us that "God created human beings, male and female, in the divine image God created them." (Gen. 1:27) Thus God contains both a masculine and a feminine side, and each side is best imaged for us in the faces of the men and women who love us the most.

The three of us experience the differences between men and women described above. For example, when we pray with a person who is grieving for a loved one, Matt places more emphasis than Sheila on separation between the living and the deceased. Although Matt will assure the grieving person of eternal connectedness with the loved one through the Communion of Saints, Matt will stress the need to also "let go" of that loved one. Sheila, however, places more emphasis on connectedness with the deceased, assuming that a person who feels securely connected in an ongoing relationship will be strengthened enough to naturally "let go" of the physical presence of the deceased.

Similarly, we tend to pray differently with a person who is angry. For example, when Linda was angry at a relative who sexually abused her (see Introduction), Dennis saw Jesus as calling Linda to forgive her relative. In seeing a God who stood beyond Linda and asked her to change, Dennis was emphasizing God's transcendence. Sheila, however, saw Jesus being angry on Linda's behalf. Linda's anger was actually expressing the anger that Jesus within Linda wanted to express. In seeing a God who lived right within Linda's present experience and who affirmed Linda exactly as she was, Sheila was emphasizing God's immanence. Since sometimes the next loving step in healing prayer may be an invitation from either Matt and Dennis's more transcendent perception of God or from Sheila's more immanent perception of God, we prefer to pray in teams. When we integrate our different ways of perceiving God, we discover

> "a mingling of the categories of the transcendent and the immanent. The result is a more complete image of God's being as a presence that is both powerful and vulnerable. We discover the falsity of the old polarization of transcendent-immanent: in fact, they are two ways we experience God's otherness."[32]

As we learn from one another to appreciate and integrate both the masculine values of separation and the transcendent nature of God, and the feminine values of connectedness and the immanent nature of God, God heals our sexual identities and makes our ministry more whole.

Healing of Adolescence

Sexual hurts are only one of the many hurts that strike during the turbulent teenage years. In a recent survey, teenagers coming to a university outpatient clinic listed as their most common hurts: failing grades on a report card (34%), arguments between parents (28%), serious illness of a family member (28%), breaking up with a boy or girlfriend (24%), arguments with siblings and parents (21%), loss of a close friend (17%), and stress from personal illness or injury (16%).[33] Many teenagers try to dull the pain by turning to sex, drugs, and alcohol only to find deeper problems that make accidents, homicides, and suicides the three leading causes of death among those fifteen to nineteen years old.[34] When adults are asked about the most unhappy or stressful time in their life, they usually pick the teenage years.

But the good news is that the stress of the teenage years can be healed to produce a healthy adult. Dr. George Valliant's survey of 100 Harvard men even found that a stormy adolescence boded well for a well adjusted adult.[35] Another twenty-year study followed 618 Hawaiian children living in poverty or disrupted homes. As expected, many of these children had a difficult adolescence and 15% even had a record of serious or repeated delinquency. But to their surprise, the researchers found that the majority of these troubled youth turned into mature adults. "Even one-fourth of the 'high-risk' youth—those whose records showed at least four 'risk factors' by age ten—developed into stable, mature, and competent adults."[36] The resilient youth, unlike their troubled peers, "had faith in the effectiveness of their own actions" and were able to take in love from elders and friends. These resilient teenagers probably also had Erikson's basic foundation of trust, since most of the mothers described their teenagers as active, affectionate, cuddly and goodnatured infants.

Healing can also come to those teenagers who are not so resilient or who have unusually severe hurts, even when the origin of the hurt is unknown. For example, eighteen-year-old Kim had repeated mental breakdowns requiring hospitalization. Kim's mother did not know what had happened to hurt her daughter so deeply. While Kim was hospitalized in a psychiatric ward, her mother asked the six women in her prayer group to pray for Kim at Eucharist. They divided Kim's life into six chronological periods, beginning with the womb. Each person "took" Kim to Eucharist during a different period of her life, asking Jesus to heal any hurts Kim suffered during that time. Three

days later Kim was released from the hospital. She remained well, married, had children, and now, fifteen years
later, is still free of mental illness.

Recently I (Matt) prayed with twenty-two-year-old
Cindy who, unlike Kim, knew very well when her hurt began. When Cindy was fifteen, she felt so discouraged by
problems with her parents and boyfriend that she attempted suicide by a drug overdose. After ten days sus-
pended between life and death in an ICU unit, Cindy
recovered but went into a lingering depression. She also
heard voices, hallucinated and was even diagnosed as
schizophrenic. Cindy was mired in identity confusion, and
unable to finish school or hold a job.

Since she had problems with her parents and boyfriend, I knew Cindy's image of God might be damaged
and might need some attention before we could pray for
healing. But she told me that recently she herself had discovered that her confusing view of God as distant, with
two signs: "Do Not Disturb" and "No," was true of her
parents but not of Jesus. Thus, when Cindy finished speaking, I said, "Would you like to pray for healing?" She answered "Yes," and I asked, "When do you think Jesus met
a person like you?" We prayed and received the scene of
Jesus praying for Jairus' dead daughter (Lk. 8:49–56).

Since her suicide attempt, Cindy had felt like Jairus'
daughter, dead inside and needing to be called back to life.
As Cindy took my hand, we asked that she feel the strong
hand of Jesus calling Jairus' daughter back to life. Then,
when Cindy was secure in knowing the hand of Jesus that
could unconditionally love her through anything, she entered into her lowest moment: her terrifying memory of the
drug overdose. She struggled because at times the fear and
pain seemed to engulf her more deeply than the reality of
Jesus' love. But as Cindy hung on to Jesus' hand, she knew

Jesus would never let go of her hand and she felt life flood back into her. Cindy could experience the lowest moment in her life and know the love of Jesus more deeply than any pain or fear.

This experience of unconditional love through healing prayer changed Cindy. The hallucinations and voices vanished. She finished school, began working in a hospital, and renewed contact with her parents. Jesus turned Cindy's life around by coming into the moment in her adolescence when she most needed to feel his strong hand. What Jesus did for Cindy in healing her lowest moment he also wants to do for each of us. He wants us to abandon any teenage image of God being distant like a critical or unconcerned parent. We can begin by asking, "When was my lowest moment as a teenager?" If we can't recall any teenage crises, we can ask, "When do I feel the most dead inside?" or "When is my lowest moment now?"

Prayer of Jairus' Daughter

a. Prayerfully read or recall the story of Jesus entering into the lowest moment of Jairus' daughter and healing her (Lk. 8:40–42, 49–56). Let go of any unhealthy image of Jesus in which he is like a distant parent or teacher.

b. Let yourself become Jesus and reach out your right hand as he reached out his hand to Jairus' daughter. For two minutes, silently pour his life and strength into that teenage girl.

c. Recall your lowest moment as a teenager or in your present life.

d. Extend your left hand and imagine Jesus taking it with his right hand. Breathe in Jesus' life and strength

through your left hand. Let that life and strength fill
you in your lowest moment.

(If you are praying in pairs, let the person on the right
begin as Jesus silently giving life, while the person on the
left silently draws that life into her lowest moment. After
two minutes, reverse roles.)

Chapter 6

Young Adulthood (Intimacy vs. Isolation)

The Monster

Once upon a time there was a man who strayed from his own country into the world known as the Land of the Fools. He soon saw a number of people flying in terror from a field where they had been trying to reap wheat. "There is a monster in that field," they told him. He looked and saw that it was a watermelon. He offered to kill the "monster" for them. When he had cut the melon from its stalk, he took a slice and began to eat it. The people became even more terrified of him than they had been of the watermelon. They drove him away with pitchforks, crying: "He will kill us next unless we get rid of him."

It so happened that at another time another man also strayed into the Land of the Fools, and the same thing started to happen to him. But, instead of offering to help them with the "monster," he agreed with the Fools that it must be dangerous, and by tip-toeing away from it with them he gained their confidence. He spent a long time with them in their houses until he could teach them, little by little, the basic facts which would enable them, not only to lose their fear of melons, but even to cultivate them for themselves.

[Don McNeill, Douglas A. Morrison
& Henri J. M. Nouwen, *Compassion*]

If you could return to any age, what age would you choose? Most people choose a year in Erikson's stage of intimacy (age 18–35), when the goal of life is to lovingly share with another friendship, procreation and work. At this stage, the critical choice is between intimacy (with its virtue of love expressed in hugs, honeymoons and deep personal sharing), or its opposite, isolation. Simon and Garfunkel sang of this struggle, "If I never loved, I would never have cried . . . I am a rock, I am an island . . . and a rock feels no pain, and an island never cries."[1]

Choosing intimacy heals. To discover who has the highest immunity to the common cold, investigators have searched from submarine crews to skyscraper iron workers. To their surprise, they discovered those with the highest immunity are honeymooners. During the intimacy of a honeymoon, a deep "yes" to life encourages the immune system to fight for more life. Hugs and kisses don't transfer germs but rather kill them off. So, next time a cold strikes, cure it by a hug![2]

Hugs restore the heart's health too. Lack of hugs and intimacy, especially in situations of conflict or criticism, can trigger heart attacks by driving up blood pressure 40–50%.[3] Dr. Helsing found that widowers, suddenly deprived of hugs and intimacy, had a higher risk of death from heart disease than married men. But the widowers who reestablished intimacy by remarrying regained the lower level of risk for heart disease they showed prior to being widowed.[4] Not only the remarried have less risk of death, but Lisa Berkman's study of 700 California adults found this also true for those having intimate and firm bonds with family, friends and the church community. They had less than half the mortality rate of those without such ties, regardless of smoking, drinking, eating and exercise habits.[5] And even when it is time to die, Elisabeth Kubler-Ross finds people are more likely to move through the emotional stages of dying into the acceptance stage if they can intimately share all their feelings with a compassionate person.[6] From our first breath to our last one, intimacy heals.[7]

Because of intimacy's healing power, the age of intimacy (or young adulthood) is one of the most critical times of change, for better or for worse. At the University of California's Institute of Human Development, Jean Macfarlane studied 200 children from infancy through adolescence. Researchers then predicted that children from troubled homes would turn into troubled adults and those with a happy childhood would become happy adults. Finally, researchers interviewed their subjects again at age thirty (near the end of the intimacy stage) only to discover that two-thirds of the predictions were wrong. During the stage of intimacy, many of the unhappy teenagers became happy, mature adults and many of the happy teenagers became unhappy adults. This was especially true for boys who had been athletic leaders and for girls who had been beautiful and popular in high school.[8]

What Is Intimacy?

How do I make a smooth transition from high school's identity stage into young adulthood's intimacy stage? The key is to move from solving identity's question, "Who am I?", to intimacy's question, "Who are we?" In identity, I discover myself. But in intimacy, I risk losing and finding myself by loving another until our two selves become "we."

Men and women may struggle with the transition from "I" to "we" in different ways. Men may remain stuck in the "I" of identity, while women may sacrifice their "I" for the sake of a "we." Daniel Levinson found men during this stage focus more on a career and seek both a mentor and a special woman to help them fulfill their career dreams. At around age 28 to 33, they revise their dreams by changing jobs, mentors or even wives. Unfortunately, the most successful businessmen Levinson studied had no intimate men or women friends.[9] Men are often tempted to place career above intimacy. Women, even if they have a career, usually focus on relating intimately with family or a close friend. Women are usually more tempted, in giving themselves to another, to sacrifice their own needs and dreams.

But the words of Tevye in "Fiddler on the Roof" remind us that this is only a generalization and that either sex can lose sight of the meaning of intimacy. Tevye asks his wife, "Do you love me?" She answers by reciting all the chores she has done during the past 25 years. Tevye says, "I know. But do you love me?" True intimacy means giving ourselves rather than our accomplishments. It happens only when both people have an "I" that can dream and a willingness to let that I become a "we" of shared dreams as they bring forth each other's gifts.

Bringing forth each other's gifts happens with the three of us. For example, Dennis is more the optimist and I (Matt) am more the pessimist. Dennis thinks he lives in the best of all possible worlds. I'm afraid he's right! When Sheila and I give retreats with Dennis, he watches all the secure, smiling people in the front rows. I watch those in the back rows who go through a whole box of kleenex, run out of the room, or fall asleep. Dennis knows what Jesus is doing; I know what Jesus still has to do. Dennis needs my gift and I need his if we are going to see the whole picture. I also tend to think that healing is usually a step-by-step process over time. But Dennis thinks people get healed if you just smile at them. If his five-second smile doesn't work, he'll try the ten-second smile for desperate cases. The only thing that puzzles him is it hasn't worked on me yet. But we need each other's gifts because sometimes the Lord heals instantly and at other times healing comes gradually. As we have encouraged each other's gifts, we have also encouraged each other to take new risks. Now, when there is little time for my step-by-step process, I can pray for healing to happen quickly with all of Dennis's expectation. And Dennis can now take one step at a time when his first smile fails to heal everything. When we love another, his gifts grow and we grow into his gifts.

Sheila too has very different gifts that I need. Sheila doesn't worry about whether healing happens instantly or gradually because she believes that if you just keep loving and affirming people they will grow. But I think people also need to be challenged. Thus Sheila nurtures more and I challenge more. We experienced this one day when I was going up the stairs and a rat was coming down the stairs. I looked at that rat and raised my shoe for a faceoff. The rat, seeing that he had met a bigger rat who was not thinking of nurturing love, turned around and ran back up the stairs. I told Sheila I almost killed a rat. She was horrified. So I asked her,

> "What should you do when you meet a rat coming down the stairs?"
> "Well, you should speak gently to it and tell it to go outside."

"What if it doesn't go outside?"
"You might pick it up by the tail—but don't hurt it—carry it down the stairs, and gently put it outside."

Sheila's way of acceptance and nurturing is very different from my way of love that challenges.

But intimacy needs both nurturing that affirms and brings forth another's unique gifts as well as challenging love that calls another into new gifts. Only when a person feels affirmed can she hear and risk a new challenge. It's like getting a baby to walk. A mother and father don't start by kicking a creeping child until she tries walking. Even if the child is old enough to begin walking, parents affirm where she is—playing games with her on the floor and just loving her. Then the day comes when a mother and father can stand the child on her two feet, hug her, take a step back and hold out their hands. The child, who just wants another hug, takes her first step toward those loving arms. Intimacy needs both the accepting love that nurtures gifts and the tough love that challenges another to try new gifts.

Ways to Create Intimacy

Even one person's intimate love can deeply heal another. For example, Tom, a simple person without training in psychotherapy, worked as an orderly in a mental hospital. One of the sickest patients in the hospital, a deeply psychotic woman, had been there for eighteen years. She never spoke to anyone, or even looked in another's eyes. She sat alone all day in a rocking chair, rocking back and forth. One day during his dinner break, Tom found another rocking chair, pulled it over, and rocked along beside her as he ate his dinner. He returned the next day, and the next. Tom worked only five days per week, but he asked for special permission to come in on his days off so he could rock with the psychotic woman. Tom did this every day for six months. Then one evening as he got up to leave, the woman said, "Good night." It was the first time she had spoken in eighteen years. After that, she began to get well. Tom still came to rock with her every day, and eventually she was healed of her psychosis.

Although Tom was not trained in psychotherapy, he knew how to give what a mentally disturbed person—and all the rest of us—need most: affirmation and emotional intimacy. Studies comparing the effectiveness of various methods of psychotherapy show that the method makes little difference.[10] Studies suggest and our experience confirms that the single most important factor in effective psychotherapy is how much the therapist loves the patient, i.e., how much the therapist provides affirmation and appropriate emotional intimacy.

Our culture misuses the words "intimacy" and "affirmation." Too often, "intimacy" has only a connotation of physical sexuality. Yet the real meaning of intimacy is the sharing of heart and spirit which the psychotic woman finally acknowledged when she said, "Good night." Similarly, we misuse the word "affirmation" as if it were something we *do*, an idea promoted by many "pop psychology" books full of ideas on how to affirm ourselves and others. But affirmation is not something we *do*. Affirmation is a way we *are*. The difference between doing and being is the difference between effectivity and affectivity. In effectivity, we actively *cause ourselves to move*, in order to use a thing or a person to gratify our own needs. Affectivity, however, is a receptive capacity to *be moved* inwardly by a thing or a person, and to let that "being moved" reverberate throughout our entire emotional life. Only the person who can be moved inwardly by our goodness can affirm us. We cannot affirm ourselves; we can only receive affirmation as a free gift from another. Affirmation as a way of being and as a free gift from another is the foundation for intimacy.[11]

I (Sheila) learned the most about the meaning of affirmation from our friend, Dr. Conrad Baars, until his death a Christian psychiatrist and author. Dr. Baars found the most common emotional hurt to be a lack of affirmation. By this he meant that many, perhaps even most, people in our culture have not had their goodness revealed to them by another who sees that goodness and loves them unconditionally. And Dr. Baars believed that we cannot become our true selves until we have been affirmed. We discover who we are only when we see our goodness reflected back to us in the eyes of another who loves us. Thus, in his book *Born Only Once,* Dr. Baars writes that all of us have been born once—physically. But many of us have never had our second or "psychic birth," because no one has ever affirmed us.[12]

In another of his books, *Healing the Unaffirmed,* Dr. Baars and his colleague Dr. Anna Terruwe describe how they first learned about the need for affirmation. Dr. Terruwe had been treating a young woman for six months, using traditional methods of psychoanalysis (in which the analyst maintains emotional or "clinical" distance), but making no progress. Finally one day the young woman was brave enough to tell Dr. Terruwe how she felt. She said, "Doctor, nothing that you say has any effect on me. For six months I have been sitting here hoping you would take me to your heart . . . you have been blind to my needs."[13]

This young woman needed something very simple,

something all of us need: to be taken to another's heart and affirmed. Some people have an aching desperate need for this, like the psychotic woman in the rocking chair. Such people most likely had unaffirmed parents who could not give what they hadn't received. But all the rest of us need affirmation, too, and on a daily basis. Because my mother was mentally ill and could not affirm me, I once had an aching, desperate need myself to be taken to another's heart and affirmed. Fortunately my grandparents and others were able to do this for me, and now I experience myself as a basically affirmed person. But I still need affirmation. Thus every day when I see my goodness reflected back to me in Matt and Dennis's eyes and the eyes of other friends who love me, I know who I am all over again and I have strength for that day. When the three of us give a retreat, we have strength and courage to speak because we see the smiles on people's faces and we feel the warmth of their hugs as we enter the room. Although affirmation can mean the difference between life and death for the most severely unaffirmed, it comes down to very simple things like a spontaneous smile and a warm hug as we enter a room. Such simple things are the most basic ways of creating intimacy.

The Four Moments of Affirmation

There are four moments in the process of affirmation.[14] To affirm another, first we must see goodness in ourselves because someone has affirmed us. If we cannot see goodness in ourselves we will not see it in others. One famous psychotherapist, Dr. Muriel James, who trains many other therapists, told me she requires that each of her students get up in front of a group and brag about him or herself for five minutes. She tells them, "If you can't find five minutes' worth of good in yourselves, how will you ever find an hour's worth in your clients?" For Tom to have seen six months' worth of goodness in the psychotic woman, he himself must have received the gift of knowing his own goodness.

The second moment in affirming another is that we notice the unique goodness and loveableness of that person, and are quietly present to it. Thus Tom spontaneously noticed the psychotic woman, found her uniquely good and loveable, and was quietly present to her as he rocked along beside her. This capacity to notice goodness and be quietly present to it requires an inner stillness and rest, a receptivity to the goodness in all of creation. If we can notice the unique goodness and loveableness of a stone or a rose or a drop of water, we will be better able to notice the goodness of a person.

The third moment of affirmation is to be moved inwardly by the other's goodness and to be delighted by it, without wanting to grab or possess or change the other to gratify our own needs. Tom enjoyed rocking beside the psychotic woman without ever trying to change her or force a response from her. The delight a person like Tom feels at simply contemplating the goodness of another requires a healthy integration of all the emotions. If we repress any one of our emotions, all of our emotions will probably be out of balance. Thus, if we repress our grief we will probably feel less joy, and if we repress our anger we will probably feel less delight in the goodness of another.

In the fourth and final moment of affirmation we let our delight in another's goodness show, especially in nonverbal ways. The actual content of words accounts for only 7% of the impact of our communication; the other 93% comes from our tone of voice, facial expression and other nonverbal behaviors.[15] The care on Tom's face as he pulled up his rocking chair and the warmth in our voices, hugs and spontaneous smiles are among the most simple and yet most powerful ways of affirming another and creating intimacy.

Intimacy with Ourselves and Intimacy with Others

Since the process of affirmation begins with seeing goodness in ourselves, intimacy with ourselves is essential to intimacy with others. Such intimacy with ourselves grows as we become aware of our deepest feelings, needs, fears, disappointments and dreams. Without these awarenesses, we will not have a self to give another. But such awareness takes time and structures. That is why the three of us take the last fifteen minutes of each day to share how we saw the day one "up" moment of consolation and one "down" moment of desolation. Sometimes to help us get in touch with consolation and desolation we might ask ourselves: What moment am I most grateful for today? For what moment am I least grateful? This gives us a way to share deep feelings, or how another has gifted us, or even to reconcile misunderstandings before they grow.

For example, one time Sheila reported desolation because we spent the evening writing rather than accepting a dinner invitation. I reported consolation that we could finally stay at home and write after four days of being overextended in ministry to others. As we shared, we saw how our different views came from different family patterns. Sheila's disturbed mother had no friends who would invite the family out, whereas my best family memories are of happy times at home. Once we saw how our patterns of intimacy had different roots, we could work out some compromises that respected each other's different needs. Now, after five years of each evening sharing the day's high and low points with each other (and if necessary reconciling any misunderstandings), we have begun to experience the commitment Erikson describes as central to intimacy. Erikson says, "One can often be 'in love' or engage in intimacies, but the intimacy now at stake is the capacity to commit oneself to concrete affiliations which may call for significant sacrifices and compromises."[16] Thus "intimacy" is not a synonym for sexual expression or romantic sharing but refers to personal disclosure and mutuality shared across a range of relationships—friendship, family, work collaboration, community living, etc.[17] As the three of us share our consolations and desolations around everything from our friendships to our work collaboration, we grow in knowing ourselves and each other.

Others also find, as we do, that intimate sharing gives them life. I notice that, regardless of what problems people bring, I often pray the same prayer. I ask God to show them one person with whom they can continue to share and who can pray with them. If a person can share and pray with a friend, that person can grow in the midst of any problem (unless it requires professional help). For married people, ideally the sharing can be done with the spouse as encouraged by Marriage Encounter, an excellent program for growing in marital intimacy.

What Keeps Marriages Together?

In the United States, where one in two are divorced and the average marriage lasts only 9.4 years, marital intimacy is a matter of life or divorce.[18] To find out what keeps marriages together, Drs. Jeanette and Robert Lauer studied 300 couples still happily married after fifteen or more years together.[19] Fewer than 10% thought good sexual relations kept their marriage together. Instead, they pointed to intimacy as the cement of a happy marriage. "Jen is just the best friend I have. I would rather spend time with her, talk with her, be with her than with anyone else."[20] After being friends and liking a person, the third quality chosen was the commitment Erikson stresses.

> 'Commitment means a willingness to be unhappy for a while,' said a man married for more than twenty years. 'I wouldn't go on for years and years being wretched in my marriage. But you can't avoid troubled times. You're not going to be happy with each other all the time. That's when commitment is really important.'[21]

The chart below ranks these 300 couples' responses to the question of what keeps marriages going. Note how these men and women have shared so much that even their top seven responses are the same.

WHAT KEEPS A MARRIAGE GOING?[22]
Here are the top reasons respondents gave, listed in order of frequency.

MEN	WOMEN
My spouse is my best friend.	My spouse is my best friend.
I like my spouse as a person.	I like my spouse as a person.
Marriage is a long-term commitment.	Marriage is a long-term commitment.
Marriage is sacred.	Marriage is sacred.

We agree on aims and
goals.
My spouse has grown
more interesting.
I want the relationship to
succeed.
An enduring marriage is
important to social
stability.
We laugh together.
I am proud of my spouse's
achievements.
We agree on a philosophy
of life.
We agree about our sex
life.
We agree on how and how
often to show affection.
I confide in my spouse.
We share outside hobbies
and interests.

We agree on aims and
goals.
My spouse has grown
more interesting.
I want the relationship to
succeed.
We laugh together.
We agree on a philosophy
of life.
We agree on how and how
often to show affection.
An enduring marriage is
important to social
stability.
We have a stimulating
exchange of ideas.
We discuss things calmly.
We agree about our sex
life.
I am proud of my spouse's
achievements.

If husband and wife share intimately with each other, their children too will grow in intimacy. Two of our friends, Mary Lou and Gene Ott, found they needed to pray together an hour each morning if they were going to successfully raise ten children.[23] During that hour, they shared with each other how they were feeling, listened to scripture, shared their reactions, and prayed with each other for whatever the other asked. Their hour brought them so close to each other that they decided to give each child an hour each week just to be intimate in whatever way that child wished—a walk, going out for ice cream, help with homework, etc. On Friday the children can invite all their friends over for pizza. Because of the love in that family, the whole neighborhood comes.

Although the Otts took an hour, even a few minutes of sharing can create deep intimacy. We chose to end this chapter with a five-minute couple prayer because so many couples drifting apart have revived their love for each other by praying this prayer regularly together. Although intimate sharing is important every day, it is especially important to celebrate special occasions. For example, one couple holds hands each wedding anniversary and shares with the whole family what they cherish in each other. They do the same for each child on her birthday. Another family shares every New Year's how they have received life from each family member and then they ask forgiveness for any hurts. This gives them so much life that even when the children are away at college they continue this New Year's custom in letters to each family member. Whatever the structure, intimate sharing keeps marriages and families together.

Healing Our Negative Memories

As we begin to build a foundation of intimate love, we can bring that love into our negative memories, just as Jesus brought intimate love into the negative memories of the disciples at Emmaus (Lk. 24:13–35). But how do we find the negative memories that prevent intimacy? When intimacy is wounded, we feel its opposite—isolation. Deaths, divorce, moving away from friends, sexual hurts, betrayal, or any deep hurt from a friend can make us withdraw from future intimate friendships.

When I (Matt) ask myself, when did I feel most isolated, I would answer, at age seven, after the death of my three-year-old brother John. His death left me with a fear of getting close to people lest they, too, leave me as John did. Although I grew up in a healthy family, John's death caused me to withdraw in some of the ways typical of those in dysfunctional families, such as an alcoholic home. I tried to please even those I disagreed with, drowned my feelings in work, and felt distant from people.[24] Even during my early Jesuit life I was afraid to make close friends. But the depth of the wound surfaced only when in confession I shared the trauma of John's death with my novice master. I found myself saying what I had never faced before: "I feel terrible over the death of my brother John. I don't feel that I loved John enough or took good care of him. I wish I could live those three years again to really love him in ways I didn't before he died." I cried and couldn't go on because I finally had brought before Jesus' love the part of myself I disliked the most, the part that had never been reconciled with my brother's death. My novice master smiled and said that Jesus was rejoicing. Suddenly Jesus' smile was within me, and as I forgave myself, I felt as though a huge concrete shell had burst open, giving me new freedom to love and be loved rather than just to dislike myself.

Finally able to like myself, I found it easy then to make close friends. For instance, later I invited seven Jesuits to three days of sharing. During these three days each of us shared for several hours the consolations and desolations of the past year so that we might see more clearly how to give and receive love in the future. These three days gave us so much life that we decided to do this each year, and we have now met annually for eighteen consecutive years.

Not only hurtful memories such as John's death, but family patterns also shape intimacy patterns. If we can relate well with all the members of our family, we will usually be able to relate well with others like them. The ideal is to be from a loving family of about one hundred kids and to be the fifty-first child, with forty-nine older brothers and sisters and fifty younger! Then we would learn many ways of relating to older and younger men and women. An ideal marriage is to get the oldest brother of many loving younger sisters married to the youngest sister (of another family!) who has many loving older brothers. Because they have loving relationships with people like each other, they have a life-time preparation for matching in marriage. But if they had difficulties with their own families, they will probably bring the same family patterns into their marriage. To find the negative pattern that hinders intimacy, simply ask, "With whom in my family did I have the most difficulty relating?"

In my family I was close to Dennis, who is only two years younger than I, so I have an easy time being a brother with men. I have more difficulty relating to women because my sister is ten years younger, so I never learned to relate closely to a sister. When women get close to me, I tend to tease them as I would my younger sister. But friendship and work with Sheila have taught me new patterns of relating to a younger woman as an intimate peer. I have learned to compliment her hairdo rather than ask my usual question, "How can it take three hours (forever to me) to do your hair?" Having women friends like Sheila has healed my negative family pattern. Not only do I need to pray through negative memories, but I also need friends who will heal intimacy hurts by their special love. I also find that the closer I relate to Sheila, the closer I relate to other women as sisters. True intimacy opens me not just to one person but to a whole healing community.

Intimacy and Our Image of God

I (Dennis) found my biggest challenge in the intimacy stage was to heal my image of God. This happened when I allowed God to be at least as intimate and loving toward me as were the people who loved me the most. The following account shares how my image of God was healed, and how because of that God was able to heal much of what had blocked me in being intimate with others (especially my German self-righteousness).

Until three years ago, my biggest block to intimacy was my German self-righteousness which always pointed accusing fingers at others. I recall, for instance, getting annoyed at how impersonally the U.S. border patrol would treat the Mexicans. One day while in California a mile from the border, I was writing outside with Sheila. We could see that the border guards would soon catch five people. We wanted to reach out to the Mexicans in some way, so we went inside, gathered up enough granola bars for them, and went out to the beach. But by the time we arrived, the five Mexicans had their hands up in the air and were being searched. We had just come from Mexico where many of our jobless friends were unable to provide adequate food for their hungry families and thus we understood why many Mexicans were fleeing. But the border guards continued to treat their prisoners impersonally—never asking who they were or why they had come. I was so upset at the guards that even though they addressed me several times in a friendly manner, I refused to communicate with them. All I could do was offer the Mexicans our granola bars and apologize for the impersonal way the border guards were treating them.

Arriving back home, I could smell the quiche Matt was making us for lunch. I told Matt what had happened and asked him why he hadn't come. Matt said, "Dennis, you were so angry at the border guards, I wouldn't have gone anywhere with you." Matt had spoken the truth. I was right in being angry at how impersonally the guards were treating the prisoners. But I was wrong in acting out that anger and treating the border guards in the same impersonal way. In refusing to communicate, even when the guards spoke to me in a friendly way, I had cut off the possibility of influencing their behavior in this daily repressive situation. So, once again we loaded up with granola bars. This time, we went to the border guards and apologized for treating them so impersonally. As we ate granola bars together, the border guards eventually shared how they didn't like capturing jobless Mexicans. But they needed their guard jobs to support their own families. The more intimately I got to know the border guards, the more shame I felt over my self-righteousness that had treated the border guards so impersonally. As I asked forgiveness for my German self-righteousness and for treating them impersonally, they were able to also open themselves to suggestions we had for treating Mexicans more personally.

What Will Happen to Robert if He Takes His Own Life?

Although I had prayed for years for a healing of my German self-righteous attitude that so often kept me from intimacy with others, the major breakthrough came five years ago when my image of God was healed. That happened when Hilda asked me for prayer because she was worried about her suicidal son, Robert. Much to my surprise her question was not, "How can I help him now?" (Later I discovered that Hilda had received counseling for the past several years and was making much progress in relating in healthy ways to Robert, even though her son seldom responded.) Rather, the fright on Hilda's face, the sleepless nights and the weight loss came from her question, "What will happen to Robert if he takes his own life?" So I asked her what she thought would happen. Hilda then went through an endless list of her son's crimes. Her list included not only murder and pushing drugs but also what she thought was the greatest crime—her son didn't want anything to do with God. Hilda said, "Since his life is only God's to take, and since he would have no time to repent of his great sins including the great sin of suicide, God would probably condemn him to hell. There would be no way I could ever help Robert again."

I did not know what to say. Like Hilda, I was taught that anyone dying unrepentant and with such serious sins would be condemned by God to hell. So I asked Hilda to close her eyes and imagine that her unrepentant son had just committed suicide. Then I asked her what she saw. Hilda said she could see Robert approaching the judgment gates where God and St. Peter were waiting to condemn him to hell. Then I asked Hilda to share if she could feel what her son felt. "Robert feels so worn out. He has gone through so much pain and hurt." Then I asked her, "What do you want to do as you see your son coming?" Hilda answered, "I want to run down and hug him and hold him close to me forever." With that she extended her arms (as if throwing them around Robert's shoulders) and began to cry. Later I asked Hilda, "Do you think God loves Robert as much as you do?" When she nodded, I asked, "Then what do you think God would do if Robert were coming down the road?" Hilda smiled and said, "God would do the same thing I did." Then she closed her eyes again and watched as God ran down the road to meet Robert and hug him. What Hilda saw was no different than the story of the prodigal son, where the father ran down the road to intimately embrace his worn out and hurt son. Scripture is full of such welcomes. Whether in the case of the unrepentant Paul who had arrested and murdered many of Jesus' followers (Acts 9:1–10) or that of the demoniac who was so closed-hearted that he asked Jesus to leave him alone (Mk. 5:7), God is always breaking through to unrepentant and closed-hearted people like Robert (Mt. 5:44–46, Rm. 5:7–8).

I had seen that God desired intimacy and loved Robert at least as much as Robert's mother did. Years later I would discover that this prayer with Hilda radically healed me because it healed my image of God. I now saw God as desiring intimacy and loving me at least as much as the person who loved me most. This meant that God would treat me at least as intimately and lovingly as Matt or Sheila or someone else who loved me deeply. But to love at least as intimately as Robert's mother loved her son or as Matt and Sheila loved me would mean that God too would never judge me with vengeance, God too would never calculate my merit on the basis of my sins, and God too would always forgive me even before I asked for forgiveness.

How Do We Read the Scriptures about Punishment?

Though Hilda's prayer and my new image of an intimate God would gradually unfold, my first reaction to the intimate way God embraced Robert was shock. So I questioned God. "What about the scriptures that tell me you punish the unrepentant sinner in hell?" God's answer left me even more shocked. "Dennis, you'll have to stop reading the scriptures." "But, God, how can I? The scriptures are your word." "That's right, Dennis, but not the way you read them."

Through my prayer with Hilda, it seemed to me that God was inviting me to listen to scripture in a new way: to hear a loving God addressing me in lover's language. For instance, God was inviting me to watch the way lovers use punishment language. I had no trouble with "punishment" that was therapeutic, such as a mother telling her overtired child, "If you don't stop fussing, I'm going to have to send you to your room for a nap." But how did God expect me to understand lover's language when speaking of vengeful punishment such as sending unrepentant sinners to hell?

One day when I heard my sister, Mary Ellen, use vengeful punishment language with her son, David, I finally understood how God could use lover's language. Mary Ellen was patiently waiting for two-year-old David to put away his toys so David could go on the weekly shopping trip he enjoyed with his mom. But David, anxious to leave, stopped with only half his toys picked up. Mary Ellen said, "David, if you don't pick up your toys, Mommy is going to have to leave you at home by yourself." David, afraid of being left home alone, picked up the rest of the toys and a moment later was ready to go shopping. Because Mary Ellen wanted so much to have her son David go with her, Mary Ellen had used what if taken literally was rejection language ("if you don't pick up your toys, Mommy is going to leave you") involving vengeful punishment (two-year-old David being left home alone).

But I knew that because Mary Ellen loved her young son so much, she would never leave him at home alone. However, if Mary Ellen were a child abuser, I would take her words literally and believe that she would leave her child home alone. But God is no more a child abuser than

Mary Ellen. Could it be that when my sister, God, or other lovers use vengeful punishment language, the threatened vengeful punishment is given not because the person has any intention of carrying it out, but only to indicate how important it is to obey so that they can love each other more? The test I now give myself to discover whether I am properly understanding a scripture passage is to ask myself the question, "When someone who loves me intimately is loving me the most, would that person act in this way?" If so, I am probably understanding that passage. If not, I am probably making a mistake, such as taking something literally which is really intended as an image.

My slowness in understanding that scripture is full of images in lover's language was nothing new to Jesus. Jesus spent a good part of his life trying to show the priests, scribes and pharisees that the scriptures spoke a lover's language which they frequently misunderstood by interpreting it literally. So, for instance, Jesus constantly struggled with them as they literally interpreted the law and the vengeful punishments regarding such things as the sabbath observance or rules for cleanliness. Thus Jesus was always in trouble with them for such things as healing on the sabbath or touching an unclean leper. That Jesus did not read scripture and God's vengeful punishments literally is perhaps best exemplified in the story of the adulterous woman (Jn. 7:53–8:11). In that story the pharisees, in quoting the law of Moses, literally interpret the scriptures in which God actually commands the vengeful punishment of death for an adulterous woman (Lv. 20:10, Dt. 22:21). If Jesus, like the pharisees, read scripture's vengeful punishment passages literally, he too would have had to join the pharisees in stoning the adulterous woman. In inviting the pharisees to put down their stones, he is inviting them to read scripture's vengeful punishment passages as he does, not literally but as one reading the words of a lover. Down through the centuries interpreting all of scripture literally has led to many abuses, such as the imprisonment of Galileo or support for slavery.

Perhaps the time I saw the greatest abuse of reading all of scripture literally was the day I visited my jailed friend, Bill, because he had just attempted to gouge out his own eye. By the time I reached Bill, the guards had chained his arms and placed him in solitary confinement because they thought he was crazy. Looking at his blood-stained shirt, I asked Bill why he had tried to gouge out his eye. He repeated to me, "If your right eye should cause you to sin, tear it out and throw it away; for it will do you less harm to lose one part of you than to have your whole body thrown into hell." (Mt. 5:29) I was struck by how crazy Bill had become by taking the first part of that passage, "if your right eye should cause you to sin, tear it out and throw it away," so literally. But then I realized that I had spent most of my life acting almost as crazily because I had taken the second part of that passage, that God would throw my whole body into hell, so literally. The truth of the matter is that the instruction to "gouge out your eye" is not to be taken any more literally than is the statement that "God will throw your whole body into hell."

What about Judgment and Hell?

As the intimate God I discovered in Hilda's prayer became more and more real to me, so did such realities as judgment and hell. Before that prayer, I had pictured myself coming up to God's judgment throne and having God with St. Peter check out the record book where all my unrepented sins would be written. But judgment for Hilda's the prodigal happened most deeply in a loving embrace. Only when in the embrace of God's love do I know the depth of my single greatest sin—the turning down of God's love.

I could hear the truth of Matt's judgment about treating the border guards so impersonally because I could smell the quiche that Matt had baked for us and experience his intimate love that would never reject me. Being filled with Matt's intimacy even as he judged my behavior, I wanted to bring that intimacy to the border guards and ask them to forgive me. God's intimate judgment empowers me to repent and change, just as does the judgment of others intimate with me, because it is given in the midst of an embrace that will not let go of me regardless of what I do. Thus God's love, just like Matt's, is not dependent upon me having repented, rather it is what empowers me to repent and even become aware of sins that previously I was unable to see—like treating the border guards impersonally. This is the meaning of 1 John 4:19, "We love because God first loved us."

Hilda's prayer not only changed what I thought about judgment but also about hell. I had thought God would send "big" unrepentant sinners to hell. But as I saw Hilda embrace her "unrepentant" son, I began to wonder. Now I am convinced that God's embrace, like Hilda's, would endlessly try everything from embraces to exorcism in order to heal Robert. Thus the only way for Robert or for myself to be eternally unrepentant in hell would be for us to forever keep saying "no" to the new initiatives of God and of those who love us most. C. S. Lewis was correct when he said that if anyone became permanently shut off in hell, the door was closed by that person from the inside, and not by God from the outside. In other words, if anyone is in hell, it is not because God sent that person there, but because that person chose it. Whether anyone will resist the love of God forever is a question we can't answer.[25] Thus the Catholic Church teaches that heaven exists and that we know at least some of the people (saints) who are there. But while the Catholic Church also teaches that an eternal hell exists and it is possible to go to hell, neither Jesus, nor the Church after him ever stated that anyone is in hell.[26] What the Catholic Church says is how Hilda invited me to live: do not judge who is condemned (Mt. 7:1–2) but pray for all to receive God's love.

Perhaps next year when I return to the Mexican border, I will again judge that the border guards are treating the Mexicans impersonally. But hopefully my judgment will not be vengeful and vindictive as before when I separated myself from the guards and rejected them because of their behavior. Rather, I hope I can share granola bars with the border guards. I hope as I share with new guards how last year's guards had to forgive my impersonal reaction, that the new guards will become open to suggestions on how they might treat the Mexicans more personally.

What the border guards and Hilda taught me is: I become like the God I adore. For years I adored a vengeful God who pointed fingers and could even send people to hell. Just as over the years I have taken on so many characteristics of my parents—when people talk to me on the phone they think I'm my dad—I had also taken on what I thought were God's characteristics. But when the God I adored became intimate and no longer pointed a vengeful finger, I became more that way too. We should pray for the gifts of intimacy that Erikson describes in this stage. But maybe for many like myself, we can only become as intimate with others as we are with the God we adore.

Prayer for Healing Intimacy

One of the best ways we have found to experience intimacy with both God and others is the "Silent Couple Prayer" introduced on page 176. In this prayer, we simply become Jesus for the other person, and silently fill that person with God's love. We find this prayer not only heals physical and emotional hurts, but also teaches people that they can give God's intimate love. Thus at healing services we often invite people to form groups of two's and pray this prayer. After a recent healing service, our friend Ann came to us and shared that during the Silent Couple Prayer the tumor in her uterus had become smaller and the pain she had felt for several weeks diminished. We encouraged Ann to ask her family to continue praying with her for a few minutes every day.

The tumor in Ann's uterus was not her only problem. Ann's relationship with her husband Jim had been troubled throughout the fifteen years of their marriage. Ann was seriously considering divorce. Two of Ann's children, Kevin and Patrick, have epilepsy and the struggle to find treatment for their seizures had exhausted the family's emotional and financial resources. Ann worried constantly about Kevin and Patrick, and her biggest fear about her tumor was her fear of what would happen to them if she died of cancer.

Four months after she attended our healing service, Ann told us the following. Although Jim had never before been open to shared prayer, he and the children lovingly prayed with Ann each day for three weeks. Ann then went to her doctor. He could not explain why her tumor was gone and why her tipped uterus had returned to normal position. With the Christmas holidays approaching, the family became busier and tapered off their habit of daily prayer. Ann's pain returned, and she asked Jim and the children to begin praying with her once again. After several more weeks of daily prayer, Ann's pain disappeared completely. Her tumor is gone, her uterus remains in normal position, and her surprised doctor has cancelled plans for surgery.

But Ann's tumor is not the only thing in her life that has been healed. Both Kevin and Patrick are on medication for their seizures, but have had none of the usual side effects since the family began praying together. As Ann allowed her children to become Jesus for her in prayer, she became aware of how God protects them and can work through them, and her over-protective fear of leaving them has disappeared. Perhaps the greatest healing in Ann's life is her relationship with Jim. Since they began praying the Silent Couple Prayer with each other their physical, emotional and spiritual communication improved so much that instead of considering divorce Ann now says, "No matter what happens, we know we can go through it together." For Ann and Jim, their God was no longer distant and uncaring but intimate enough to heal a uterus. As the God they adored became more intimate and healing, for the first time in their marriage Ann and Jim became that way for each other. Healing came to their marriage as they became like the God they adored.

Shortly after Ann's family began praying together, the National Epilepsy Foundation chose nine-year-old Kevin as Poster Child. The family gave press interviews, went to Washington to meet the President, and spoke at Epilepsy Foundation meetings. The new peace and joy in this family has been so evident that Ann receives many letters from troubled epileptics and their families, asking how they too can live peacefully and joyfully with the ordeal of epilepsy. Ann shares with them the power of the following simple prayer.

Silent Couple Prayer

You may wish to pray this way for a few minutes each day with your spouse or another person with whom you have a primary relationship.

a. Get in touch with how you need Jesus' help.

b. Share it with each other.

c. Let one person give prayer and the other receive. If you are giving prayer, get in touch with your love and God's love for the other person. Reach out as Jesus within you wants to reach out and simply fill the other for five minutes. The person receiving prayer simply breathes in love.

d. Then reverse roles.

(If you are alone, imagine yourself holding hands with Jesus and a person who loves you. For five minutes breathe in their love for you. Then, ask Jesus what the person who loves you most needs. With Jesus (or Mary) breathe Jesus' healing love into that person.)

Chapter 7

Adulthood
(Generativity vs. Stagnation)

The Holy Place

Time before time, when the world was young, two brothers shared a field and a mill, each night dividing evenly the grain they had ground together during the day. One brother lived alone; the other had a wife and a large family. Now the single brother thought to himself one day, "It isn't really fair that we divide the grain evenly. I have only myself to care for, but my brother has children to feed." So each night he secretly took some of his grain to his brother's granary to see that he was never without.

But the married brother said to himself one day, "It isn't really fair that we divide the grain evenly, because I have children to provide for me in my old age, but my brother has no one. What will he do when he's old?" So every night he secretly took some of *his* grain to his brother's granary. As a result, both of them always found their supply of grain mysteriously replenished each morning.

Then one night they met each other halfway between their two houses, suddenly realized what had been happening, and embraced each other in love. The story is that God witnessed their meeting and proclaimed, "This is a holy place—a place of love—and here it is that my temple

179

shall be built." And so it was. The holy place, where God is made known to his people, is the place where human beings discover each other in love.

[Belden C. Lane, "Rabbinical Stories"]

Erikson calls the period of middle age the stage of generativity, and he places it approximately from age 35 to age 65. When the three of us speak about the period of middle age during a retreat, we often ask how many in the group are middle-aged. Most people groan loudly and raise their hands slowly. The groans assume that to be middle-aged is to be "over the hill." Yet many hands go up because especially at this stage people seek the inner growth in wholeness and in self-giving love found at retreats and workshops. Although we may dread becoming "middle-aged," we also admire those who exemplify this stage's virtue, care.

Gandhi—Model of Generative Care

Erikson too admired those who exemplify this stage's virtue, so much so that he wrote an entire book about Mahatma Gandhi and his gift of generative care.[1] To win independence from the British, Gandhi taught the Indian people that when non-violence is based upon care and inner strength, it is the most powerful form of resistance. Gandhi wanted the British to leave India, but he wanted India and Britain to part as friends. Gandhi succeeded. In 1946, the British left peacefully and granted India independence. Then, however, the two major groups in India, the Hindus and the Moslems, began to compete for political power. Gandhi, himself a Hindu, believed the most truly powerful Hindu response would be to freely give away government offices to the Moslems. But Gandhi's people could not go quite that far with him, and chose instead to divide India into Moslem and Hindu territories through the partition of Pakistan. As refugees moved from one territory to another, civil war broke out between Hindus and Moslems. The Indians, who had peacefully defeated the British, were now killing each other.

Gandhi, heartbroken, declared a fast and vowed not to eat until the killing stopped. One scene in the movie "Gandhi" shows him when he has been fasting a long time and is very weak. A group of Hindus comes to visit him, and one young man pushes through the crowd. His wild eyes are full of despair and anger. He throws a piece of bread on Gandhi's bed and yells:

Hindu Man: Eat! I am already going to hell and I don't want your death on my soul too.

Gandhi: Why are you going to hell?

Hindu Man: Because I killed a child. The Moslems killed my son and so I killed one of their children. I smashed its head against a wall.

Gandhi: I know a way out of hell. Find a Moslem child the same age as your son, whose parents have been killed in this war. Adopt that child and raise him as your own. But be sure you raise him as a Moslem.[2]

At this, the man collapses on Gandhi's bed. Gandhi lays his hand on the man's head, as if pronouncing absolution. When the man rises, the wildness has left his eyes and he leaves peacefully.

This scene from Gandhi's life illustrates what Erikson

means by generativity and care. Generativity includes care for others beyond one's family, for future generations, and for the kind of world in which those generations will live. As the Talmud says, "Three things one should do in the course of one's life: have a child, plant a tree and write a book."[3] Although a common way of generativity is through parenting children, other ways include the roles of teacher and mentor, or any other way of creating life and passing it on. For example, Matt and Dennis and I generate life through giving retreats and writing books. Matt and Dennis also experience generativity by living in a Jesuit formation community and supporting younger Jesuits preparing for priesthood, and I (Sheila) by visiting Matt and Dennis's community and relating to them in ways that model healthy celibate friendship for the younger men. Although the three of us do not have biological children, we find other ways of passing on our life and its meaning to the next generation.

Confronting Inner Darkness

As adults in the stage of generativity seek to pass on life to the next generation, they may find themselves asking, "What do I really have to pass on?" As they try to answer this question, they may discover in themselves not generativity but what Erikson describes as its alternative: stagnation. Stagnation is the feeling of having forfeited my contribution to life in my age, a contribution that would have been handed down to future generations. A crisis of meaning may occur as adults like the heartbroken Gandhi discover stagnation in their lives and begin to think, "I had these dreams and they never got fulfilled. I am not doing the things I really want to do. I am just on a treadmill, keeping in motion but not receiving life or giving it. I haven't put my stamp on anything. Time and energy are running out. I have to take a different direction or my life will continue hollow and empty." This search for a deeper and more meaningful way of living often involves a confrontation with inner darkness, as it did for Gandhi.

During his fast Gandhi faces a crisis meaning and confronts inner darkness. Gandhi had given his life to teach his people forgiveness and peace, and now they are bitterly accusing and killing each other. Rather than blame his people, Gandhi looks at himself and asks, "What have I been living for? Was it worth it? How have I failed?" Gandhi resolves to face the darkness in himself, and his fast is a way of doing penance for the violence and any way he himself contributed to it.

Gandhi's life became an example for the entire world of what Erikson means by generativity and its virtue of care. Even in the midst of his own crisis of meaning, Gandhi still tried to pass on life and be a mentor for the next generation. When the young Hindu man came to him, Gandhi cared for that man by teaching him that forgiveness and loving care for others are the only way to be free. Gandhi cared not only for people of his own religion and social class, but for all of India. Although he came from an upper class Indian family, he associated freely with untouchables. He shocked his sexist culture by trying to treat women as equals. Gandhi's care extended even beyond his own country, as when he said, "We want the British to leave, but we want them to leave as friends." During the struggle for independence from the British, Gandhi led the Indian people in a strike against buying British cloth. Then, when Gandhi visited Britain, he went to see the millworkers and apologized for any way the strike was hurting them. Gandhi's example of caring beyond himself and the way in which he resolved his "crisis of meaning" affected the course of history for the entire world.

Adult Crises

Although Erikson was one of the first to recognize adult crises, now others are writing about how adult growth continues through many crises.[4] Adults face the loss of aging parents, a job change or retirement, children having problems or leaving home, marital difficulties or even divorce, an aging or ill body, financial problems, and especially the mid-life crisis question Gandhi asked, "What do I really have to pass on?"

The "mid-life crisis" is misnamed because it can happen any time and many times, whenever we question the meaning of our life. Twenty percent of us will never have a mid-life crisis, whereas many people have one every six to eight years. These crises are brought not so much by years as by the number of transitions faced (e.g., job change, kids gone, breast removed, death of a loved one, etc.). Thus a crisis of meaning can occur at any age, but is most common during the forties, when you first realize there are more yesterdays than tomorrows. You begin to ask, "What do I still want to do before I die?" You feel you are no longer growing up but growing older and you count not only birthdays but also how many years you have left. All your curves are in the wrong places, you squint through bifocals, and you don't count your projects in terms of hours but in terms of how much energy it will take to finish them. So, the good news: all of these "crises" are "normal." The bad news: you might have many "normal" times.

Such normal mid-life crises may take a different form

in men and women. Carol Gilligan finds that women tend to develop from caring for others' needs (e.g., raising children) into caring for their own needs too (e.g., starting a career after the children are grown). Men, however, tend to develop in the opposite direction, caring first for their own needs (e.g., sacrificing relationships to advance in their careers) and only later caring for others' needs.[5]

Solution = Caring

Both men and women resolve mid-life crises by finding new ways of caring for oneself and others. Erikson sees the virtue or task of care as finding the balance between generativity's giving to others and self-absorption's receiving for oneself. The person who just gives to others risks burn-out, smothering others, and an empty inner life.* The person who just receives risks self-centeredness, indifference to others, and never becoming an adult who generates life. As Jesus said, the ideal is to love one's neighbor as oneself (Mt. 22:39). Loving oneself means taking time for the inner journey through solitude, intimate relationships, recreation, hobbies, retreats, prayer, journaling, exploring new areas of learning, etc. In this way the uncared for sides of the personality grow: the thinker becomes more feeling, the introvert more extroverted, and the critical judge perceives more openly. Men develop their feminine side (anima) and become nurturing cooks, receptive to music and affectionate with children and grandchildren. Women de-

---

*When caring for others is not in a healthy balance with caring for self, we can fall into any of the following distortions of caring: 1) doing for others what they can do for themselves, 2) giving help others don't want or need, 3) giving help I don't want to give, and 4) I or the person helped expecting something but not asking for it.[6]

velop their masculine side (animus) and become educated, initiating, and more assertive and sure of themselves. After my parents had raised our family, I (Matt) watched my father take up art and my mother go back to school to learn a new way of caring as a developmental reading specialist. To avoid or solve the mid-life crisis, we can simply ask, "How have I failed to care for myself and my undeveloped side?"

Caring for myself is only half the solution because it can become a self-absorbing, stagnating focus without generativity's reaching out to care for others. Jean Vanier, who has founded over two hundred L'Arche homes for the retarded and handicapped, discovered why some communities grow in love and have a waiting list of eager volunteers, while other communities fall apart.[7] Vanier found the communities that grow have both sides of generative care: care for oneself and care for others. Care for oneself comes from having the intimate love of at least one friend with whom one can share everything. So in each community Vanier places one or more mature, generative people who can provide friendship. But Vanier also found that communities with only friends still stagnated. He noticed that besides a friend, a community also needs at least one difficult person who calls others to grow in unconditional love. Scripture focuses on such love, using the word *agape*, meaning unconditional love even for one's enemy, 250 times. Perhaps you are lucky in having more than one person calling you to unconditional love!

Often the person most difficult to love is the person most different from us. The conservative administrator who wears a belt and suspenders will be driven crazy by the iconoclastic artist who wears practically nothing at all. But a community needs both those who preserve tradition and those who creatively dream. True community happens not where all think the same but where differences are respected. Thus psychiatrist Scott Peck in his study of community says that a community passes through four stages: "pseudocommunity," where members pretend all is well and avoid conflict; "chaos," where members express differences but try to obliterate the other's differences or seek a dictator who won't allow differences; "emptiness," where members put aside their ideologies, prejudices and expectations to understand the different world of another; and finally "community," where people with their differences are accepted and loved even if not always liked.[8] If it sounds difficult it is, and that's why we must be filled with a friend's love or we will have no love to give the difficult person.

How do we work out the balance between receiving love from friends and giving love to those in need? Five years ago, our friend Joe began going to Alcoholics Anonymous. After several months, Joe stopped drinking. Joe wanted to share with his old drinking friends the healing he had received. He began reaching out to them and encouraging them to join A.A. But soon Joe was drinking again, joining his old friends in the bar instead of them joining him at A.A. meetings. Joe's A.A. sponsor and community reached out to him and helped him recover from his relapse. Joe became an active A.A. member, eventually sponsoring many others. We asked Joe how he would know if he were ever in danger of another relapse. Joe told us he would know he had stopped growing and was in danger if he ever stopped reaching out to other alcoholics. In the beginning of his recovery, what Joe needed most was care for himself, and he was not yet ready to care for others. As Erikson and A.A. observe, one must accept one's identity (in Joe's case, as an alcoholic) and have intimate relationships (for Joe, the commitment of his sponsor and community) before one is ready for generativity.[9] Five years later, Joe needs most to reach out and care for others. The reaching out that in the beginning brought a relapse now brings Joe ever-deepening healing. Caring is in the proper balance to the degree we give and receive new life.

Where Do We Start to Care?

Where can those in the generativity stage begin to reach out and care? One way is to begin as A.A. does, by reaching out where we ourselves have received some healing. For example, seven years ago George felt he had failed as a father when his son was imprisoned on drug charges. George determined to be a good father not only to his son but to many other fatherless prisoners as well. Even after his son was released and doing well, George and his wife Lucy kept visiting their other imprisoned "sons" and "daughters." This gave George so much new life that he eagerly trained in A.A., opened his home as a half-way house, and has helped many prisoners find sobriety, jobs—and a caring father.

Another example is Fr. Ken Leone's parish of 8,000 people, one of the most alive parishes in the Denver area. This parish has sixty-eight different ministries, yet Ken attends only one meeting per week at which he encourages the ministry leaders. Ken's other evenings are spent celebrating home Masses, where he finds the ways family members have let hurts become gifts and leads the family in affirming each other. Then Ken invites them to use their gifts in the ministries of the parish. For example, a loving couple who once fought continually, now does marriage counseling. Another couple, who had grieved the loss of their child, now works with grieving parents. Thus, healed hurts become gifts of compassion.

Besides starting with the gift we have from healed hurts, we can start with the person we love. For years I heard about massive problems of war, world hunger, etc. that seemed too big for me to do anything. Knowing all the grim statistics made me even more concerned about all the problems. But I was not caring compassionately because the problems were statistics and not people I loved.

Concern sees the problem, while compassion says, "I just can't let that happen to my sister or brother." Two years ago the three of us lived in a Guatemalan village where half the children die from malnutrition or other diseases before age five. Yet the villagers eagerly provided free food and housing to the 7000 who came to our retreat. We were hugged by people who had walked for twenty-four hours and could hardly stand up. Yet in their weakness as they prayed for physical healing for each other, deaf ears, crippled legs and painful backs were healed. As they prayed for reconciliation, soldiers who had participated in murder and torture asked forgiveness of their victims' survivors. Villagers who, under torture, had given out names of fellow villagers sought and received forgiveness from those they had betrayed. One ragged old woman told of finding the mutilated body of her abducted husband in a ditch. She shared how God had touched the agony in her heart, given her peace and helped her forgive the murderers. Suddenly the statistics of war and hunger had faces and they were my sisters and brothers who could love more deeply than I could. We no longer had to convince ourselves we *should* care but now gave our time and resources because we *wanted* to love and be with friends. Because they were in our hearts, we could make a life-changing decision—to study Spanish in Bolivia for six months and then do more Hispanic ministry. The Guatemalans who loved us moved us from passive concern to active compassion.

The greatest Christian saints have known that this active compassion is the heart of the gospel. Once, the destitute mother of two Franciscans came to St. Francis's monastery to beg food. The porter told St. Francis, "There is nothing in the house to give. The only thing of value is the scriptures [copied by hand]." Francis answered, "Then give it to her. It is better to practice charity as we are told by the scriptures than to keep reading the scripture and not practice it."[10]

Generativity and Intercessory Prayer

One prayer that expresses the gift of this stage is intercession. To intercede in a lifegiving way, we first need a listening heart that listens to how Jesus compassionately cares for the person. Sometimes, if we don't understand that person, we can ask Jesus to help us become like that person and experience whatever will help us grow in compassion. For instance, Leo wanted to pray for his senile father Frank, who would wander around Chicago thinking he was actually back in the Mexico of his childhood. When Leo prayed, he adjusted his whole posture to be like Frank's, even stiffening his fingers to experience Frank's arthritic hands. Leo also allowed his heart to begin feeling the concerns and worries that Frank felt most when disoriented by senility. After the prayer, Leo told us that he really did become like his father, and experienced Jesus and some other unknown person love him. When Leo returned home, he found that Frank's senile behavior had disappeared. Four years later, Frank still remains well. Another friend, Helen, prayed for her ninety-year-old father who for years had been waiting to die. She prayed by becoming like her father and releasing herself into God's arms. At that moment her father, who was 1000 miles away, died peacefully. Both Leo and Helen's prayer had such power because they tried to compassionately intercede like Jesus who, as high priest, interceded by becoming like us in all things but sin (Heb. 2:17, 4:15).

Prayer of Releasing Another

Sometimes when we intercede for another, that person is already too entwined around our heart and we become drained. Then we need not to enter her world more but rather to release her. The release prayer is important for me because after I lovingly pray with another, I can become a burden bearer wanting to do more for a person than I can do. At times like this, I need to release the person and her problems into the hands of Jesus.

One midnight Jesus taught me the power of physically releasing a problem into his hands. After a full day of workshops, I had just dragged myself into the chapel for a quick prayer before bed. As I rose to shuffle off to my room, I heard a woman crying. I wanted to bury myself in sleep but realized that I would just lie awake wondering about her. So, in my own self-interest, I asked Joan if she wanted to talk.

For twenty minutes, Joan poured out her worries about her daughter, Mary Ann: Mary Ann's husband drank and had run off leaving the bank ready to foreclose on their home, her two sons had high fevers, the baby in her womb was in the wrong position for birth, etc. I told Joan that we couldn't do anything for her daughter who lived five hundred miles away. I suggested that Joan just pray aloud, placing her daughter in Jesus' hands. So Joan prayed forever (at least twenty minutes), telling Jesus all her worries about her daughter. But as soon as Joan ended the prayer, she began to cry again. Joan still held her daughter locked in a worried mother's heart.

I didn't know what to do next but in desperation (and my own need for sleep) I said, "You did well on describing the problem to Jesus but not so well on releasing her into Jesus' hands. This time, let's begin by cupping your hands, holding your daughter in them, and offering her to Jesus. Then pray again *briefly*, telling Jesus how your daughter needs his care. But this time release your daughter into Jesus' hands. Be brief because Jesus has already heard everything twice!"

Joan prayed interminably again, squeezing her hands around her daughter and telling Jesus all Mary Ann's problems. Then Joan took a deep breath and opened her hands wide as she released Mary Ann to Jesus. After that prayer I was exhausted and grateful to finally get to bed.

In the morning Joan tried to find me and I tried to avoid her because I didn't know what else to do for her. In the afternoon she trapped me and said, "I tried to find you because Mary Ann called this morning. During the night her husband came home and he wants to go to Alcoholics Anonymous for help with his drinking. My two grandsons awoke with no fever. The bank called and can extend their loan. She even thinks the baby is repositioned for a normal delivery." I could hardly believe it, but five out of Mary Ann's eight problems had been solved that night as we simply released her into Jesus' hands. Jesus wants us to do what we can for another and then release the rest into his hands.

Parents especially need to do what they can and then

let Jesus heal the mistakes every parent makes. When parents attend our retreats, they often say, "If only I hadn't made that mistake with my child, he would be ok today." (See Appendix B.) What harms the child most is not the mistake but rather not being taught how to grow from mistakes. Many of my fellow Jesuits grew up in alcoholic families just like those that damage many children. But these Jesuits were blessed as their parents found A.A., asked forgiveness for past mistakes, forgave themselves, and taught their children to trust God as much as they did to be Savior. Jean Vanier has also found that a suffering child needs not perfect parents but rather parents who ask forgiveness and seek God's care together with their children.

> . . . it is indispensable that parents do not stand alone in front of their child. If they are alone the child identifies them as the source of everything, as God: he or she makes them idols that are worshipped rather than icons which signify the presence of God. The child is unable to accept that not everything in its parents is good. If, however, parents introduce their children to the mystery of God, the child will discover that parents are not alone and all powerful; they are not the prime source of life; they can have their faults. The parents are then able to ask forgiveness of their child when they make mistakes. The child and parents are together before God as brothers and sisters, praying and asking forgiveness together.[11]

Usually we can forgive ourselves only after we have forgiven our own parents for being hurt and human rather than God. The problem isn't making mistakes but rather not trusting one's mistakes to a God who heals and whose infinite care can create new life in any time of hurt.

Discerning How to Care

If we are not finding new life, how do we discern where Jesus is calling us to care more for ourselves or for another so we can find new life? My mid-life crisis came at thirty-four, when I (Matt) was struggling between two choices I didn't want: staying on the Sioux reservation to teach religion or leaving the reservation to give healing prayer retreats. I didn't want to stay because half my students had quit my religion class when they were given a choice between taking religion or basketball, their favorite sport. The other half, whose parents insisted they take religion, wanted to quit my class when they heard the others bouncing basketballs in the gym next door. But I also feared giving healing prayer retreats because I have no special gift of miracles or of hearing Jesus through the word of knowledge. When I close my eyes and ask for a vision, all I see are my eyelids. In healing prayer I would have to depend on God to act. I felt uncomfortable being that dependent on God, and I feared that until God acted people would be in total chaos having nervous breakdowns and climbing walls. Although I researched and wrote down all the reasons for staying and for leaving, my fears would not let me freely choose one or the other.

God had a plan for freeing me to choose. One night I was driving next to a cliff when a drunken driver began weaving down the hill toward me. To avoid him, I turned too far off the road toward the cliff's edge. Fortunately, my back bumper hooked on one lonely guard post that swung the car around and back up on the highway but facing the wrong way. Amazed that I could move, I got out of the car and stood on the highway. I moved my arms in gratitude for life given again to me after I had been certain I would end up either dead or paralyzed. I was grateful for everything; even the $600 dent in the car was beautiful because it had saved my life. I was so grateful to God for having saved my life that I just wanted to offer my life in service in whatever way God desired.

To my surprise, I found that I could now gratefully choose anything God wanted because now even breathing reminded me of how God gifted me. The next day, eager to teach, I told Jesus that I would teach forever if necessary. No longer looking for results, I only wanted the chance to serve and return God's gift of life. My fear of healing retreats also disappeared. I knew that if God could rescue me from falling down a cliff, God could also rescue any retreatants who started climbing the walls. I was so much in touch with God's love that I finally voiced a deep "Yes, I will do whatever you wish." That "yes" resounded deeper than any of my fears. Perfect love from knowing God's care does cast out fear and gives freedom to find God's will.

In deciding whether to teach or give retreats, how then did I finally go about listening to God within me? Since both now seemed like good choices, I didn't immediately know which to choose. In my prayer I imagined returning to the moment of my deepest "yes." Once again I felt the gratitude inside myself as I looked at the $600 dent and felt how my life belonged to God. Then, still imagining myself standing on the highway, I matched both possibilities against my deepest "yes." My deepest "yes" resonated most with surrendering to retreat work, making me even more dependent on God than teaching did. This choice of retreat work was confirmed as I consulted with those who loved the Lord and really knew me, including my superior.

He scared me by asking me to go into retreat work with Dennis full-time for at least ten to fifteen years. All my fears surfaced again and so once more in prayer I stood on the highway. I found that my superior's request again matched my deepest "yes" better than did the part-time retreat work I had wanted. By returning to the moment of my deepest "yes" to God's care and then consulting those who love God and know me, I can always test whether I am hearing God's will. The final test for God's will is whether living it out brings life to me and to others.

The more we give retreats and write books, the more we generate life in ourselves and in others. Ten years ago, Dennis and I gave retreats where we just prayed for everyone to be healed. Now on retreats, Dennis and Sheila and I are teaching people how to develop their own gifts of prayer and healing. Our last three books and this book can all be used in small group courses so people can pray with each other and do the very things we do. (See Appendix C.) The three of us began these courses when we entered the stage of generativity, but without realizing as deeply as we do now that the ideal of generativity is not just to care for others but also to mentor others so they develop their own gifts and no longer need us. Generativity discerns caring choices and knows the parable, "Give a man a fish and he eats one day. Teach a man to fish and he eats a lifetime."

Ready to fish?[12]

Saying Yes to the Future

a. Recall the moment in your life when you felt the most loved, when you most wanted to say "yes" to life. Reexperience that moment and whatever was said or done that made you feel so loved. Breathe that love into your-self again, and with it the longing to say "yes" to any place in life where you can give and receive love and pass on life to others.

b. As you look forward to the rest of this year, get in touch with a way Jesus may be calling you to give life in a new situation. Tell Jesus anything that makes you feel hesi-tant about this new situation. As you picture the new situation, breathe into it the power to say "yes" or "no" to it in whatever way Jesus is leading you.

Chapter 8

Old Age
(Integrity vs. Despair)

The following prayer was found at the Ravensbruck death camp where 92,000 women and children died. It was scrawled on wrapping paper near a dead child.

Lord, remember not only the men and women of good will but also those of ill will. But do not only remember the suffering they have inflicted on us; remember the fruits we have brought, thanks to this suffering—our comradeship, our loyalty, our humility, the courage, the generosity, the greatness of heart which has grown out of all this, and when they come to judgment, let all the fruits we have borne be their forgiveness.

Recently some friends of my parents died. When I (Dennis) asked if their friends were old, my parents responded, "No, they were only in their early seventies." As my parents get older, I notice that their criteria for old age changes. My parents and others living in Erikson's final stage (sixty-five years or older) may be happy to find out that Erikson calls his final stage not only "old age" but also the "age of integrity" or the "age of wisdom."

Last Christmas while at home, I found my parents doing many of the tasks which Erikson suggests will bring integrity and wisdom. Since we had given them three empty photo albums for Christmas, we all began sorting through bags of photographs. We had separate piles for their parents, their own baby pictures, their school and childhood friends, their wedding, their children including myself, and the biggest pile of all for their grandson, David. Each evening we would turn on the tape recorder and have them talk about the memories that one stack of photographs recalled. My dad, for instance, spoke of how his family struggled to keep their farm during the Great Depression. Tracing his family back to early eighteenth century farmers, he spoke about how his family always treasured the earth and how even today the easiest way for him to begin working through anxiety or depression is to dig around in his garden. No wonder today in my room I am caring for the plants of sixteen students away during school vacation.

As we listened to my dad speak of his past generations and their care of the earth, we were all experiencing one of the attributes Erikson suggests for integrity or wisdom in old age. "It is a sense of comradeship with men and women of distant times and of different pursuits, who have created orders and objects and sayings conveying human dignity and love."[1] Besides a comradeship with the past, Erikson suggests that integrity and wisdom also mean acceptance of one's own life. "It is the acceptance of one's own and only life cycle and of the people who have become significant to it . . . free of the wish that they should have been different, and an acceptance of the fact that one's life is one's own responsibility."[2] What struck me as my parents spoke was their ability to look back and find how they had grown through everything. They did not wish that "things should have been different." Whether it be the Great Depression when their families had pulled together and shared, or the death of my brother John that had opened their hearts to adopting my sister Mary Ellen, they shared how seeming tragedies had become a source of their growth.

How Can Anyone Choose Wisdom in a Concentration Camp?

If my parents had not been able to see tragedies like the Depression or my brother's death as sources of growth, they would probably be wishing their lives had been different and experiencing what Erikson says is the alternative to wisdom: despair. In contrasting wisdom and despair, Erikson emphasizes that wisdom is more like gratitude or hope, rather than just a knowledge of many things. Perhaps the choice between wisdom and the alternative of despair is best exemplified by the story of Wild Bill, a prisoner held in a German concentration camp. Most prisoners thought that Wild Bill had arrived recently because he seemed to have endless energy, working eighteen hours a day. But others knew Wild Bill had lived for six interminable years on their starvation diet and in their disease ridden barracks.

Before his imprisonment, Wild Bill lived in Warsaw's Jewish ghetto with his wife, three sons and two daughters. Before Bill's eyes, the Nazis shot his sons, daughters, and wife. Brokenhearted, Bill begged the soldiers to kill him too rather than exile him to a concentration camp. But because he knew six languages and they needed a camp interpreter, the soldiers did not kill him. Wild Bill describes how his reaction changed.

> I had to decide right then whether to let myself hate the soldiers who had done this. It was an easy decision, really. I was a lawyer. In my practice I had seen too often what hate could do to people's minds and bodies. Hate had just killed the six people who mattered most to me in the world. I decided then that I would spend the rest of my life—whether it was a few days or many years—loving every person I came in contact with.[3]

Wild Bill poured his love out in six languages for eighteen hours a day to reconcile arguments whenever they arose among the different nationalities in the camp.

When Wild Bill decided that the tragic killing of his family by Nazi soldiers would not make him a hater of soldiers but rather a camp reconciler, he moved from despair toward integrity or wisdom. Erikson suggests that despair ordinarily begins with contempt of individuals (e.g. the soldiers who killed my family), then encompasses institutions (e.g. this concentration camp with disease ridden barracks and starvation diet), and finally leads ultimately to contempt of oneself (e.g. begging the soldiers to kill me too).*

On the other hand, tragedy leads to Erikson's wisdom or integrity when it leads someone like Wild Bill to start to construct the meaning of his life. Thus Wild Bill determines to "love every person I come in contact with" and to be a camp reconciler. For Erikson, to construct such meaning one has to acknowledge one's diminishments (e.g., Wild Bill having his home, family, and freedom of movement taken from him), forgive others (e.g. Nazi soldiers), forgive oneself (e.g. Wild Bill's second guesses on how he could have responded differently before, during or after the day the Nazi soldiers came), and thus accept the fact "that one's life is one's own responsibility."[4] Thus the gift of wisdom and integrity happens as we or Wild Bill discover the gift and meaning buried deep within any tragedy or life experience.

The disciples on the road to Emmaus experienced this same movement from despair to integrity and wisdom with Jesus (Lk. 24:13–35). The despairing disciples began by talking about the tragic death of their friend whom they had counted on to be messiah. The disciples' attitude was, "Don't talk to us about God's wisdom. We haven't seen much of it in our meaningless life or in the death of our friend." Jesus simply shared from Scripture and showed how even the experience of their friend's

---

*Despair can also *begin* with contempt of ourselves. That would happen, for instance, if in an abusive situation such as Wild Bill's, we blamed ourselves for feeling anger or hatred. The example of Wild Bill is not meant to discount anger at injustice or hatred of evil, when inflicted on either oneself or another. We find meaning in tragedy not because we lack appropriate anger and hatred, but rather because we do feel anger and hatred, and we let ourselves be loved and empowered in the midst of our feelings.

death was to be life-giving, part of the wise plan that God had for their lives. In the stage of integrity, nothing— even death itself—is able to rob us of being a wiser and more gifted people.

Choosing Wisdom in Diminishment

Erikson's final stage of integrity challenges Wild Bill, the Emmaus disciples and ourselves to not only find gift in the death of those we love but also to find the gift as we face our own death and the diminishments that old age brings. A study ranking traumatic events in old age lists first, death of a spouse, then being put in an institution, the death of a close relative, major personal injury or disease, and finally losing a job and divorce.[5] Erikson expands on this list and describes how the elderly can experience diminishment in each of life's eight stages. "Old patients seem to be mourning not only for time forfeited and space depleted but also . . . for autonomy weakened, initiative lost, intimacy missed, generativity neglected—not to speak of identity potentials bypassed or, indeed, an all too limiting identity lived."[6] An unknown senior citizen described this world of diminishment.

Everything hurts and what doesn't hurt doesn't work.
The gleam in your eye is from the sun hitting your bi-focals.
You feel like the night before and you haven't been anywhere.
Your little black book contains only names ending in M.D.
You get winded playing cards.

> Your children begin to look middle aged.
> You join a health club and don't go.
> A dripping faucet causes an uncontrollable bladder
>   urge.
> You look forward to a dull evening.
> You need glasses to find your glasses.
> You turn out the lights for economic rather than
>   romantic reasons.
> You sit in a rocking chair and can't get it going.
> Your knees buckle but your belt won't.
> Your back goes out more than you do.
> You have too much room in the house and not
>   enough in the medicine chest.
> You sink your teeth in a steak and they stay there.
> You know all the answers, but nobody asks you the
>   questions.

Regardless of what the diminishment is, integrity and wisdom come as a result of not only mourning the diminishment but ultimately finding the gift in it. While learning Spanish in Bolivia, I (Matt) lived with a family whose father, Julio, slowly died of leukemia. But each week as he lost more control, he became more grateful for the little that was left. For instance, when the medicine burned his throat so he could hardly utter one word, each word meant more. His most common word became "gracias" (thank you). He stuttered a gracias when he could keep down one crust of bread or wake out of a coma. To utter one word, eat one mouthful, or awaken for an hour was no longer taken for granted, but all became gift. He reserved the deepest "gracias" for tightly holding, as if for the last time, the hand of a friend. Each night he also grasped my hand with more love and both of us had greater desire to never let go.

In the final moment of his death, each family member held his hand tightly and hugged and kissed him. Although Julio vomited blood, deliriously shoved a daughter away, or went into an unresponsive coma, nothing could stop the family from loving their father. The weaker Julio grew, the more they loved him. I knew God could be no less loving. Even if Julio were to deliriously push not just his family but even God away, God would embrace him with at least as much love as I saw his wife give in her last embrace. Seeing and feeling such great love, I no longer needed to die the perfect death, pronouncing "Jesus" with a smile on my face. I no longer feared dying deliriously and even denouncing my friends and God. I knew that the love of my friends and God would overcome any way I might push them away. Since Julio's death, I count not on my control but on their love growing more deeply with every diminishment as I let go into the Hands that never let go.

What Do I Need to Do Before I Die?

In the age of integrity I face the fact that like Julio, I am soon—sometime anyway—going to die. I then begin doing important things that answer the questions: "If I only had until Christmas to live, what would I do? What is really essential in my life? What do I need to do before I die?"

The sooner we ask, "What do I need to do before I die?", the more meaning our remaining life will have. It is never too late to change life's direction as did Alfred Nobel, founder of the Nobel Prize for the greatest achievement in the arts and sciences. As a Swedish chemist, Nobel amassed his fortune inventing dynamite and explosives ideal for weapons. When his brother died, a newspaper accidentally printed Alfred's obituary. Thus Alfred had the unique opportunity to read his own obituary in his lifetime and to see how posterity would remember him. He was shocked to read that he was remembered for making a fortune by enabling armies to achieve new levels of mass destruction. He then determined to change his life's direction before he died. We remember him today because shortly afterwards he used his fortune to found the Nobel Prize, which annually rewards the research that most benefits humanity.[7]

Like Alfred Nobel, most people need to live in some new way before they can peacefully die. As a way of freeing people to fully live so they could at last peacefully welcome death, our cousin Sr. Mary Jane Linn wrote *Healing the Dying*, based on her experience of caring for 150 of her retired sisters, whose average age was eighty-two.[8] In her book she describes how many of these aging sisters, who for the past ten or fifteen years had been waiting to die, finally became free to die. Each morning Sr. Mary Jane would simply ask God to tell her what a given sister still needed to do before dying. Then Mary Jane would help the sister do it and often found that the sister was able to die a few hours or several days later. Sometimes, for instance, Mary Jane would find that she needed to listen and write down a sister's entire life story. Once the sister knew that someone understood her life and that it was written down, not only would she be freed from compulsively retelling that same story, but she would also be free to die within a few days.

Fr. Robert, who had read Sr. Mary Jane's book recounted how when he helped a woman give away all her possessions, she became free to die. The woman, Kathy, suffered intensely from cancer pain and longed to die. Because she had lived a long time on social security, she found herself with fewer and fewer possessions but valu-

ing each one more. But the breakthrough in releasing herself to die came when under each treasured possession she
put someone's name and why she wanted that person to
have it. I asked Fr. Robert what Kathy left for him. He said
a major turning point happened in Kathy's life fifteen years
earlier when she made a pilgrimage to Rome. Thus while
in Rome, she bought a cross that would be a constant reminder to her of the new life she received on that pilgrimage. Fr. Robert held up the cross and said to me, "Kathy
wanted to give me this cross because she said I helped her
on her second pilgrimage, the pilgrimage toward her
death." I asked him, "To how many people did she specifically give something?" He said, "Between 100 and 150.
She had something marked for almost every person who
attended her wake. When Kathy had made sure she had
left something for everyone, she could die."

When Mary Jane showed me several of the life stories
her sisters had dictated to her, or when Fr. Robert held up
the cross Kathy left for him, I understood better what Erikson describes as the "end of life" crisis. This crisis is "a
new edition of the identity crisis which we may state in the
words, 'I am what survives of me' "[9]. Perhaps the person
I have seen work hardest to leave a legacy that would survive him is my friend Bill Carr who was dying of cancer.
For months Bill and his wife Jean worked on what would
be his final project, a videotape series called *Dying to Live.*
(See Appendix C.)

In this series of videotapes, which has a half hour on
each of Jesus' seven last words, Bill shared what he was
doing about each word so that he too, like Jesus, could release himself to die. For instance, after hearing Jesus' first
word, "Father, forgive them, they know not what they
do." (Lk. 23:34), Bill shared how he made a list of fifty people. Since each person on his list was someone that either

he needed to forgive or who needed to forgive him, Bill bought a van and went and visited nearly all fifty people. Thus each of Jesus' last words helped Bill to take care of some unfinished business.[10]

In the stage of integrity, the more we come to terms with our life's unfinished business, the more we can welcome the greatest diminishment: death. At the end of Bill's videotaped conference, Bill told us what sums up a wise person who has lived well the age of integrity: "I love life and there is much I would like to do. But this workshop is the last thing I absolutely need to do. From now on I have an open calendar."

Reminiscing With Positive Memories

Have you ever wondered how your grandparents could remember in detail events occurring 50 years ago as if they happened yesterday? Psychiatrist Robert N. Butler, who has written extensively on topics related to aging, believes this experience of reviewing one's life is universal among older people.[11] He sees the reminiscing so characteristic of later years as a looking backward which is set in motion by looking forward to death. While some functions of the mind become less sharp with old age (abstract thinking as in math and physics), other functions of the mind usually become sharpened, such as the ability to reminisce and make sound judgments based on remembered life experience.[12] It is as if nature equips us to integrate life by remembering experiences to garner wisdom rather than despair. The elderly also instinctively know the wisdom of beginning with positive memories of "the good old days," because negative memories without love's positive foundation can lead to despair, the trap of this age. So also in this book, at each of the eight stages we began the task of accumulating wisdom and integrity by first of all recalling positive memories before healing any negative ones.

Who Are the Most Alive Elderly Persons I Have Known?

Besides having positive memories from every stage of our own life, we need positive memories of seeing others growing old. I can ask myself, "Who are the most alive elderly persons I have known?" Just being with or recalling how they embraced life to its last breath removes despair's fear of growing old. For example, in her advanced years Agatha Christie wrote her mysteries and married the famous archaeologist Lord Mallowan. She embraced life and said, "It's wonderful. The older I get, the more interested he is in me!"[13]

I also think of our friend Herman Scott whose jolly laugh always alerted us to his arrival. Until age 45 Herman worked a Minnesota dairy farm to care for his invalid mother. When his mother died, Herman sold the farm and moved to St. Louis. He spent nothing on himself, lived in one tiny room, slept on mended bed sheets discarded by a hospital, and refused any welfare or social security payments because he thought these should only go to the poor who can't care for themselves. Even though he lived simply, thieves constantly broke into his room. Finally, Herman discovered trust was the only way to keep thieves out. Thus when leaving in the morning, he would prop the door wide open with a chair on which he would put this sign: "Art, welcome! Sit down and have a beer from the refrigerator. I'll be back in five minutes. Herman." The fictional Art never appeared but neither did the burglars.

Herman, who especially loved children, even won an award for working 20,000 volunteer hours at Cardinal Glennon Children's Hospital in St. Louis. He added so much joy that when in later years he could no longer walk to the hospital, he was given a hospital room, free lunch (which he insisted on paying for), and a wheel chair so he could continue making his deliveries and bringing laughter to depressed children. Each person he helped became a lasting friend. When he died at age 80, Herman had his body donated to medical science. His body was the last thing he had to give away. His safety deposit box was already empty except for his greatest treasure, his address book of all his friends. Among Herman's friends were nearly thirty people he had put through college. Herman used all the income from the sale of his farm to make sure the poor could get the educational opportunities he himself had missed when caring for his invalid mother. Although Herman's poor lifestyle might not be lifegiving for many of us, for Herman it was the Lord's call because he continually grew in joy and the ability to give and receive love. Remembering Herman's zest for life recalls how the mystic Meister Eckhart defined wisdom: "Wisdom consists in doing the next thing you have to do, doing it with your whole heart and finding delight in it."[14] Herman's wisdom came not just from old age but from a lifetime of giving thanks and of gratefully embracing the present moment.

Giving Thanks Now for a Lifetime

Because wisdom comes from giving thanks, we can enjoy wisdom long before old age. Several years ago I (Matt) also experienced the wisdom that comes from giving thanks. This happened when I was to take final religious vows, twenty years after my first vows as a Jesuit novice.[15] I searched for a way to make my final vows mean even more than my first ones. So I decided that I would spend the year before final vows prayerfully giving thanks for the twenty years since my first vows. As I gratefully remembered the positive times (like working with the Sioux) and healed the negative memories (such as being misunderstood) until I could be grateful for these memories too, I was filled with new life and energy. Although I usually find writing for more than two hours difficult, after being filled with gratitude for my past twenty years, I had so much energy that frequently I could write for hours, even past midnight. Because I was looking gratefully at how Jesus was with me in the past and present, on vow day I knew Jesus' commitment to me and eagerly committed myself to our future together.

Right after vows my friends started commenting, "You are going to be forty in a month, aren't you? It's too bad your life is half over. Are you ready to be forty?" Then they shared all the aches and pains they had after forty and how the body goes downhill. I began to feel old and think, "I can't remember names any more. I've forgotten all my Spanish. My body is declining—I get tired faster and I need bifocals. It's bound to get worse rather than better." As I focused on my limitations, my energy evaporated and I lost all creativity to continue writing.

Then I stopped and thought, "What's going on? I'm only three months older than I was when I took my vows and felt wonderful. The difference isn't age but attitude. When I took vows, I was grateful for ways I had received life in the past and knew God would be as faithful in the future. But when I turned forty, I looked only at limitations and what could go wrong. That's the only difference." As soon as I began to gratefully see how God was working or could work in any situation, new life again pulsated in me. Now every night I go to bed grateful for something that has happened during the day and wake up filled with more life. Since my vows I have been living one scripture verse. "Rejoice always, never cease praying, give constant thanks for that is God's will for you in Christ Jesus." (1 Thes. 5:16–18) And, by the way, life gets better after forty.

Integrity Beyond Death

Matt was able to experience integrity and wisdom as he turned forty in part because he had models of integrity and wisdom in his life, such as his parents and Herman. In each stage of development, the virtue of that stage is not our own achievement. Virtues are a gift to us from those more mature people around us, especially our parents, who model them for us and who provide an atmosphere in which we can "catch" them. Thus, for example, in the story of Andy and Karen and their children (pages 60–61), Susan and David "caught" healthy autonomy to the extent it was present in their parents.

But many of us do not have parents like Andy and Karen, or like Leonard and Agnes May Linn. As we look to our parents for an example of virtues such as wisdom, we seem to find only despair. We may wonder, "Will I do any better than my parents? Will I be like them when I am old?" As the three of us visited Leonard and Agnes May last Christmas and listened to them share memories into our tape recorder, I (Sheila) was aware of how different it would be if I asked my own mother to share memories.

As described in Chapter 2, my mother suffered all her life from what seemed a form of minimal brain damage or chemical imbalance. Her physical symptoms included such poor motor coordination that she could not do even simple housekeeping tasks. Her emotional symptoms were like those of a psychopathic person, in her seeming inability to feel empathy, guilt or remorse. Thus, rather than reflect on the meaning of her own experience and take responsibility for her life, she blamed all her problems on others. Thus my mother could not be an example for me of Erikson's stage of integrity.

If my mother had been my only source of motherly love, the hurt of her illness might have destroyed me. But fortunately I was loved by my grandmother and other healthy women, so that I had the psychic strength to survive my mother's home, to search for healing of the hurts I experienced in that home, and to let those hurts become gifts. I knew that I had to find the gifts in the hurt of having such an ill mother in order to find the meaning of my life and achieve integrity for myself. Gradually I saw that my sensitivity to emotional deprivation in others and how they can be helped, and my compassion for those who seem "selfish" and unloving are a gift from having a mother who could not meet my emotional needs and who seemed profoundly "selfish" and unloving.

I even had a mysterious inner sense that I had chosen my parents because only through the experience of having them as parents could I do what God had sent me here to do. I cannot explain this theologically, but I sensed that somehow God and I had talked it over before I was sent here and that I had agreed to be born to my parents for the sake of the purpose of my life. Thus, as far as I knew, I had accepted my mother as she was, accepted how her illness had affected my life, and accepted myself as her daughter. Once others had filled in the emotional deprivation she left me with, I had resigned myself to believing that I needed nothing from my mother and should expect nothing since she was so unable to give. I would have to grow in integrity and wisdom without her help.

Then, while we were still writing this book, a friend called from Oregon to tell me that my mother had died suddenly of a heart attack. I put the phone down and began to pray for my mother. Often I had prayed for her in the past and I would sense her spirit, but she would seem to me like someone in a coma. At those moments I would feel that I knew her as she really was, but that she could not respond to me. As I prayed for her on the evening of her death, I again sensed her spirit. I realized that this time her spirit was responding back to me, that *she* was praying for *me*. I surprised myself by calling her "Mama," a name I hadn't used since I was a baby. After all her years of illness, now I finally had a mother who could love me.

When I arrived in Oregon for the funeral, I went to my mother's home. I wasn't going to stay there overnight, since I had always felt uneasy in her home. I especially did not want to be there alone; Matt and Dennis and my brother and sister would not be arriving until the next day. But her home was full of peace, and suddenly I knew that she and Jesus wanted me to stay. I slept securely and when I woke up I knew my mother had been caring for me all night. The care I felt was different from what I had received from my grandmother and other mother figures; it was *my mother* caring for me.

On the morning of my mother's funeral, we went to the mortuary to view her body. As I looked at her now peaceful face, I felt a new understanding of how difficult her life had been, how courageously she had struggled to survive, and how little any of us had understood the terrible odds she struggled against. I told her I knew she had done her best, and I would do my best with what she had given me. I introduced Matt and Dennis to her and spoke

Rosabelle Fabricant.

to her about my friendship with them. I told her I could love them for her, in ways she had wanted to love her own family but couldn't. I asked her to pray for us and to care for our ministry.

On the day after the funeral, I met Wally, my mother's social worker. Wally said that during the past six months my mother had begun to reflect upon her life and see that she had lived in destructive and unloving ways. He gave me several examples of moments when she had said, "Maybe I was wrong about that," and of moments when she behaved compassionately toward others. Wally thought that what killed my mother was her chronic high blood pressure combined with the stress of her new sense of remorse. Because she was unfamiliar with remorse, she knew nothing about forgiveness either. Thus she didn't know any way to be healed of her remorse for the damage she had done to others. What moved me most was when Wally said, "When I first met your mother I didn't like her and I dreaded her phone calls. By the time she died, I loved her and I will miss her." For the first time in her life, my mother had a friend.

When I asked Wally what he thought had helped my mother to change, he spoke of his own relationship with her and of the loving community she had found at the local synagogue. Healthy in their own sense of autonomy, these people had refused my mother's abuse. Yet, filled with generativity, they had loved her unconditionally and won her trust. Later I realized that it was six months before, in June, that Matt, Dennis, myself and several of our friends celebrated a Mass of generational healing for my mother and her family.[16] Perhaps Jesus answered our prayers by touching her damaged body chemistry and by sending her a community in which she could learn to give and receive love.

As I listened to Wally, I saw that my mother, who I

thought could give nothing to me, had given me a profound example of the struggle for integrity. She had faced the considerable destructiveness of her life and accepted responsibility for it, even without the comfort of knowing that forgiveness is possible. In the midst of this confrontation with her own darkness, she made friends and laughed at herself for the first time in her life. My mother, who struggled against far greater odds than I, who am blessed with a healthy mind and body, had begun to achieve what Erikson describes as integrity, " . . . an acceptance of the fact that one's life is one's own responsibility."

Erikson also speaks of integrity as "a sense of comradeship with men and women of distant times and of different pursuits, who have created orders and objects and sayings conveying human dignity and love." As we sorted through my mother's belongings, I saw how in this way, too, my mother had struggled for integrity. She had saved everything from old family photographs to my elementary school report cards. Although my mother was so physically uncoordinated that she could not operate a vacuum cleaner, she had somehow kept in perfect condition in her living room my grandparents' lovely oriental rug. Although most of my mother's life had lacked human dignity and love, some spark of life preserved within her spirit had known a comradeship with her children and her ancestors. She had tried her best to preserve the objects that spoke to her of the dignity and love she herself lacked.

Although I never saw the changes Wally spoke of in my mother, I feel them in her presence to me through Jesus, when I pray for her. I sense that now her greatest desire is to love me, her other children, and our father in the ways she could not while she lived. The greatest gift I can give her is to receive her love, and as she grows in her new life, to allow her to be for me a model of all the virtues, including integrity. I, in turn, can help her growth as through prayer I extend to her whatever I achieve of integrity in my own life.

Thus, just as we believe Erikson's first stage begins before birth, so we believe his last stage extends beyond death. Although integrity includes accepting the limitations of our parents "free of the wish that they should have been different," we need not think our parents cease to mother and father us when they die. Not only is God our Mother and our Father; we are also held in God's heart together with our human mother and father, in an eternally growing relationship of love. When we know that even lives of tragedy and failure that seem to end in despair are not over and that growth continues for all eternity, then we can truly say with Dag Hammarskjold, "For all that has been, thanks! For all that will be, yes!"

Prayer of the Grateful Heart

a. Imagine that you are at a slide show. Watch as only pictures of the happy moments of your life appear on the screen. Breathe in once more the "yes" to your life that was in those moments.

b. As your "yes" to your own life deepens, see if some moments appear on the screen that surprise you—moments which at the time seemed meaningless or which you couldn't accept, but which you now see as gifts because of the good that has come from them. As you continue to breathe in your "yes" to the moments you see on the screen, breathe out any feelings of failure or fear that your life has been meaningless.

c. Thank God for the gift of your entire life and the way that all of it has meaning in God's eyes.

Stuck?

As blizzard winds howl outside, I hear the whining of a stuck car futilely spinning its wheels. The harder the driver tries, the more the wheels spin, digging an icy hole that further traps the car. Finally a neighbor comes and pushes the car out of the icy hole and back down the hill. The driver backs up further to the level street, then gathers enough momentum this time to make it up the hill.

While watching this drama, I saw not only how cars get unstuck but also how people do. If we have been deeply hurt, it usually doesn't help just to try harder. Our wheels spin and we get more discouraged and trapped. We usually need a loving neighbor who can guide us back to the stage of trust. Backing up, especially to positive memories, builds more trusting momentum for another run up the hill. Trying harder works to the degree it has momentum from Erikson's first stage of trust.

We gather momentum to trust when we gather positive memories and reexperience the times we gave or received love. We can begin by answering the question, "What memories make me most grateful?" Only after resting in those memories can we go on to ask, "What has happened in my life for which I am not so grateful?"

Perhaps reading this book has brought to mind negative memories where it is difficult to see or to celebrate any growth. This is good and normal. If someone robbed and beat you, would your first words be, "Praise God"? When his persecutors beat him, Jesus said, "My God, my God, why have you forsaken me?" He did not say, "Praise God." Sometimes when we have been emotionally hurt, a process of psychological healing needs to take place, just as when we have been cut, a physiological process of healing needs to take place. And if we rush the process, if we pick the scab too soon—if we say, "Praise God" too soon— we have to start all over. In her work with the dying, Dr. Elisabeth Kubler-Ross discovered five emotional stages: denial, anger, bargaining, depression and finally acceptance.[1] Although dying is the deepest hurt, we can encounter these same stages in healing any emotional hurt as we try to forgive those who hurt us. While teaching on a Sioux reservation, I (Matt) learned how moving through these five stages of forgiveness could facilitate the process of healing an emotional hurt.

One day one of the students—a senior named Jack— came charging into the class. He was drunk and he didn't know where he was. Jack was about twice my size. As soon as Jack saw me, a rage came over him. He grabbed me, began pounding me, chased me around the room and threw me to the floor. Jack's girlfriend was in the class, and she knew that he would be thrown out of school if he kept hitting a teacher. The only thing that saved me was that Jack's girlfriend came between him and me and tried to stop him from hitting me. At first Jack didn't even recognize her, and he threw her to the floor too. She got right back up and came between us again. Finally Jack realized who she was, and she was able to lead him out of the classroom.

Even after Jack left the classroom, I was still shaking. I tried to save face in front of my students by pretending that nothing had happened, but I couldn't teach at all that day. I went into a stage of denial, trying to smile and telling myself that I wasn't hurt at all. I can tell when I'm in denial because I only half-listen and I don't want to feel anything. I cover my injured feelings by working harder, and I don't take time to be alone or to pray. I worked and worked all that evening, but finally at the end of the evening I did what helps with denial.

At any one of the stages there are three things we can do: decide we want to forgive, act in a loving way, and pray for the one who has hurt us. When I'm in denial, deciding to forgive begins with recognizing that I need to forgive. The best thing for me to do is to sit down with the Lord and say, "What am I grateful for in this day and what am I not so grateful for?" That's when it came home to me that I was not grateful at all for what had happened with Jack that day. I felt that I had looked like a fool being chased around that classroom. I feared that the students would never respect me again, and I felt ashamed.

But gradually as I became less aware of feeling ashamed and more aware of blaming Jack and wishing that it had never happened, I moved into the second stage of forgiveness: anger. My feelings were all focused outward, against him. I wasn't ready yet to ask whether I had acted immaturely. I began having thoughts such as: "Jack should be thrown out of school!" Usually I don't even catch those angry thoughts, but I am getting better at catching my typical anger-stage behavior. I get "hurry sickness," where I run through yellow lights, eat to finish rather than enjoy a meal, and try to do as much as I can in as little time as possible. I jog fast because anger gets locked into my muscles and releasing physical tension helps me release emotional tension as well. But even while jogging, I compete with those around me because I am full of a floating anger that has to find some kind of a target.

Both talking to a friend and praying to Jesus about the

real target of my anger can help me drain some of it out. So I began telling Jesus about all the things that were wrong that day until I felt my anger with Jack. I shared with Jesus my anger and hatred for Jack and let myself be loved with all my feelings. I sensed that Jesus wanted me to know that he too was outraged at the hurt I had suffered. Once I knew that Jesus understood me, I began asking for Jesus's eyes, asking to understand Jack. I asked "How do you want to change him, Lord?" I had lots of ideas of how Jack should change, but as I prayed, I began to see Jack's wounds. Jack's father, a criminal who had spent his life in prison, finally killed himself. I realized that I was the father figure in that classroom. When Jack was drunk in that classroom, the anger of all his hurts from his father was directed at me. I can start to forgive people when I become aware of why they're acting as they are. They aren't out to get me but are wounded and need love. So I asked Jesus to help me pray his prayer for Jack.

When I can begin to understand why a person has hurt me by seeing the person with Jesus' eyes and praying his prayer, then I often move into the third stage of forgiveness: bargaining. Bargaining means that I will forgive people *only if* they do this or that first. These bargains that the other person change are often appropriate wishes arising from our sense of integrity that (like Jesus) is outraged by injustice and wants to keep that injustice from happening again. For example, one of my bargains was that I would forgive Jack only if he apologized for his unjust attack. My sense of integrity told me that I deserved an apology and that only by facing what he had done would Jack change his violent behavior. To move through the stage of bargaining, I did not have to give up this appropriate wish for Jack to change. I only had to become willing to forgive whether Jack changed or not.

I had two other bargains. I would forgive Jack only if, first, he stopped drinking and second, if he recognized how well I handled the situation. Bargains can come from either our strengths or our weaknesses. My first bargain came out of strength, my strength of not having a drinking problem. If I become proud and think that I'm doing it on my own strength—"If I can do it, he can do it"—then I start to demand the same thing of someone else. I demand of others the very things I am proud of, not realizing that they are gifts from the Lord. On the other hand, my second bargain, that Jack recognize how well I handled the situation, came out of my weakness. Through such recognition I wanted Jack to cover up the weakness I was ashamed of: the fearful coward running away from Jack as he chased me around the classroom and the volcano of anger that couldn't forgive once he was out the door. Before I would forgive Jack, I wanted him to tell me how much courage I had and how I controlled my anger so well. I wanted this weakness covered so that I would not have to change my volcanic anger and face my shame. Whether I am bargaining from my sense of integrity, my strengths or from my weaknesses, I need to get under the cross and say, "Jesus, help me to forgive this person, not because he deserves it but because he needs it." I shared all my bargains with Jesus, telling him all the ways I wanted Jack to change before I would forgive him. Jesus showed me how he appreciated those ways in which my bargains came from my sense of integrity and justice. Then I asked Jesus for his heart that forgives unconditionally whether Jack changes or not.

When I reached the point of beginning to cancel bargains, I moved into the depression stage. In this stage I started asking what was *wrong with me*. Why had I reacted so badly? Why had I been so frightened? Why had I let this hurt affect me for so long? Why didn't I see that Jack was after his father and not me? Why couldn't I forgive him as his girl friend did who forgave him instantly after being thrown to the floor? I realized that I had never spent any time alone with Jack getting to know him, and so, of course, I was just a blank on whom he could project his father. "I should have been a bigger and better person," I thought. When I am in the depression stage, I say "I should." When this happens, I have a choice to make. I can keep beating on myself, or I can let the Lord and others love me and forgive me. I had to choose whether I would live for the students' opinions of me, or for Jesus who loved and forgave me and wanted to help me change the things in myself that needed change. The gift of the depression stage is that it can show me ways I really do need to change. As I saw how my attitude of staying distant from people had contributed to Jack's attack, I wanted to change. As a first step I began visiting students in their homes and opened a home for students with alcohol abuse problems.

Since I let the Lord love me and help me change, I could begin to move into the fifth stage of forgiveness: acceptance. Sometimes it is difficult to distinguish between acceptance and denial. The difference is that in denial I cannot reach out to another or be grateful, whereas, in acceptance, I can reach out to the very person who has hurt me and grow in gratitude for what before I considered only a hurt. I am not grateful for the destruction I experienced, but for the new life that came from it. When I asked the Lord to help me grow in gratitude for what Jack had done, I began feeling grateful for three reasons.

My first reason for gratitude was discovering what it was like to be a Sioux. Although I had learned their Lakota language and even lived with a Sioux family one summer, the day I was chased around that classroom taught me the most about what it's like to be a Sioux. Sioux families suffer from seventy percent unemployment and rampant alcoholism. To be an Indian means to have someone out after you, whether it's a white person or another Indian—someone you're afraid of who might come home at night out of control. I had never felt their pain until I experienced in the classroom what the Sioux live with all the time.

My second reason for gratitude was that now I knew how the Sioux could live with resentments and have a hard time forgiving. I saw how long it had taken me to forgive Jack, and I stopped demanding that others forgive and change overnight. I became aware of how I had talked to other teachers about my students, pretending that it was "constructive criticism," but really just trying to make myself look good. I gradually criticized less as I saw how, in ruining a student's reputation, I had been doing to another the very thing I disliked Jack doing to me.

My third reason for gratitude was that my prayer life grew through my experience with Jack. Since I knew that I couldn't forgive Jack on my own, I knew that I needed Jesus. The biggest thing that hurt gave to me was a vision of who I wanted to be and how I needed Jesus' help to become that person. I wanted to be like Jack's girlfriend. I had seen Jesus in her. I had always known that Jesus on the cross could take any abuse and still forgive. But when I saw Jack's girlfriend love him unconditionally and forgive him instantly no matter how much he abused her, I knew that it was possible for human beings to have Jesus' forgiveness if they loved deeply enough. The example of Jack's girlfriend has helped me to ask again and again for the gift of being able to forgive and to give life to others the way she gave it to me by loving Jack so much. In this prayer I am asking for the gift of unconditional forgiveness.

A person usually goes through the five stages described above in dying or in unconditionally forgiving any hurt. The first stage is denial, when we pretend it didn't happen. The second stage is anger, when we blame the person out there. The third stage is bargaining, when we say, "I'll forgive, only *if*. . . . " The fourth stage is depression, when we blame ourselves. And the fifth stage is acceptance, when we can be grateful not for the evil but for how it has gifted us in many ways, especially in even being able to reach out to the person who has hurt us. Dr. Elisabeth Kubler-Ross first developed these stages from watching the process that dying patients moved through in finally accepting their death. She also saw patients who became stuck at a stage, e.g., remained angry and died that way. Why did some progress to acceptance and others get stuck? The main difference she observed was that all those moving to acceptance had a significant person with whom they could share their feelings and be loved. Having such a person enabled them to move from one stage to the next. The most important thing about these stages, then, is not that we remember them but that we share them with a significant person who loves us. If in prayer we share these stages with Jesus and allow him to be a significant person for us, we'll move automatically through the five stages.

(If you would like a suggested way of sharing the five stages with Jesus in prayer, or if you wish to read about the five stages in greater depth, see our books *Healing Life's Hurts* and *Prayer Course For Healing Life's Hurts*.)

Appendix B:

How Do I Help Those I Have Hurt?

When we give a retreat on "Healing the Eight Stages of Life," conscientious parents always ask us, "How can I heal the mistakes I have made with my kids?" They focus not on how their parents and others hurt them but how in each stage they made mistakes as parents. Usually these good parents realize they now have more love and wisdom than they gave their children. The more parents have grown, the more they see and regret their earlier mistakes. So if you are asking this question, give yourself credit for having developed as a parent. If you can't love yourself and see your own growth, you will not be able to see and affirm the ways a child grows.

The serenity prayer says, "Lord, give me the courage to change what can be changed, the patience to accept what cannot be changed and the wisdom to know the difference." What can I change? The easiest and most important person to change is not my child but myself. The best gift a child can have is a healthy, loving parent. Rather than worry about how to heal our children, the first step is to heal our own hurts that harmed and continue to harm them. We can begin by strengthening our positive memories and healing the negative ones that surfaced while reading this book. Perhaps if we are stuck, we might profit also from counseling or a specific group such as Adult Children of Alcoholics which helps with the patterns learned in any dysfunctional family. When we once again live a healthy, balanced life, we have life to give to those we have hurt.

Once on our feet, we can help another. For instance, often a couple growing in love notices that the last child is more secure than the first born. One such couple sat down with their eldest teenager and told her how they loved her and asked forgiveness for the specific mistakes they made in raising her. Amid a flood of tears a deeper relationship was born. It is better to make mistakes and ask forgiveness than to avoid mistakes and never teach a child how to reconcile. Real love means wanting to do more and having to say "I'm sorry." Such love also finds creative expressions. This family has collected over one hundred good video movies to lure teenage friends into wholesome fun. Another couple, as mentioned in Chapter Six, tries to spend an hour each week individually with each of their ten children. The family also has pizza night every Friday for their children's friends and this is slowly creating a healthy neighborhood. We can love our children by loving their friends who often influence them more than parents can.

But after we have tried to change what can be changed, there will still be some things that we can't change because we are not God but fallible human beings. The next step places what we cannot do in God's more powerful hands. For example, Ann had tried unsuccessfully for twenty years to help her son Tom who kept angrily withdrawing from the family. Tom had acted this way ever since his difficult birth followed by many days in an incubator. During that time Tom, alone and separated from his mother's love, struggled to survive. Now twenty years later, Tom still lived as if he had to struggle to survive alone. His mother still found that the more she tried to love him, the more Tom would distance himself. Finally Tom eagerly left home for college and had little desire to ever return.

One day Ann decided to hold Tom's photo on her heart and ask for the love of Jesus and Mary to flow through her heart and change her son. But after praying this way for several days, she discovered that Tom was only getting worse. When she asked herself "Why?", she was shocked to discover that, even while she prayed, her love was conditional on Tom's changing. She took the photo again and not only prayed for Tom to change, but also allowed Jesus and Mary's unconditional "no strings attached" love to flow through her even if Tom never changed. As she closed her eyes and prayed this time, she saw her son in a blue sweater rather than in the suit he wore in the photo. A few days later she saw this same sweater in a department store and she bought it to give Tom at Christmas.

Several months later Tom came home for a short visit and said, "I don't know why but the last couple of weeks I've been eager to spend some time at home perhaps at Christmas. Maybe you can put in a word to Santa Claus that I want a blue sweater like all the fraternity brothers have." Tom then described the exact same sweater Ann had seen in her prayer and had bought two months ago. Ann laughed and said, "We will have Christmas now!" So she pulled out from her secret hiding place, that all mothers have, the sweater Tom had just described for the first time. Ann told Tom how she saw the sweater as she prayed for him. Tom was amazed at how much God loved him, even telling Ann to get him a sweater two months before he knew he wanted it. They held each other and cried as they experienced how God was healing their relationship. Now they go for long walks together and share their hearts.

Prayer guarantees no fast or infallible solution. But if we love another with the depth of Jesus' unconditional love, our hearts—like Ann's—will change even if our Toms do not. When we pray for another, that person may receive or reject the love of Jesus. But the more we give the depth of Jesus' unconditional love, the harder it is for another's heart to keep rejecting our prayer. Even stubborn St. Augustine held out for only seventeen years when facing the prayer of his persistent mother, St. Monica. Augustine's stubbornness made Monica a patient saint. We simply pray and leave results up to God who will deepen our love and is always full of surprises. Ann never would have guessed that a blue sweater would heal Tom. So too, St. Monica prayed that Augustine would stay away from wicked Rome. But God's answer was to send Augustine to Rome where he met St. Ambrose who converted him. So if you are ready for a surprise, you might want to try Ann's photo prayer.

Photo Prayer

a. Hold against your heart a photo of a person for whom you want to pray. (If you don't have a photo, use another reminder of the person such as a letter or even his name written on a piece of paper.)

b. Ask Jesus to help you to love this person unconditionally as he does and to have his prayer for the person in your heart.

c. When you love this person with Jesus' heart, then pray Jesus' prayer or do whatever Jesus moves you to do.

Resources for Further Growth

Courses

Healing the Eight Stages of Life, by Matthew Linn, Sheila Fabricant and Dennis Linn (Mahwah, NJ: Paulist Press, 1985). Tapes and a course guide which can be used together with this book as a course in healing the life cycle. Videotape version has 12 30-minute sessions; the first 8 sessions are also available on audio tape.

Prayer Course for Healing Life's Hurts, by Dennis & Matthew Linn and Sheila Fabricant (Mahwah, NJ: Paulist Press, 1983). The accompanying book can be read as a summary of ways to pray for personal healing, or it can be used as a course of 24 lessons with journaling and prayers to bring healing. For use as a course, there are 24 30-minute sessions available on video or audio tape.

Praying with Another for Healing, by Dennis & Matthew Linn and Sheila Fabricant (Mahwah, NJ: Paulist Press, 1984). The accompanying book can be read as a guide to praying with another for hurts such as sexual abuse, depression, loss of a loved one, etc. Normally, this course would follow the more basic *Prayer Course* or *Eight Stages* course. There are 12 30-minute sessions available on video or audio tape. Our book *Healing the Greatest Hurt* may be used as supplementary reading for the last 4 of these sessions, which focus on healing of grief.

Dying to Live: Healing through Jesus' Seven Last Words, Bill & Jean Carr and Dennis & Matthew Linn (Mahwah, NJ: Paulist Press, 1983). In this set of 8 30-minute sessions on audio or videotape, the speakers present a workshop on how the seven last words of Jesus empower us to fully live the rest of our life. The tapes may be used with the book upon which they are based, *Healing the Dying,* by Mary Jane, Dennis & Matthew Linn (Mahwah, NJ: Paulist Press, 1979).

Books

Healing of Memories, by Dennis & Matthew Linn (Mahwah, NJ: Paulist Press, 1974). This book is a simple guide to inviting Jesus into our painful memories and letting him help us to forgive ourselves and others.

Healing Life's Hurts, by Dennis & Matthew Linn (Mahwah, NJ: Paulist Press, 1978). This more thorough book helps the reader pray through hurts using the five stages of forgiveness to reach the final stage: gratitude for what has happened because of the new life that has come through it.

Healing the Greatest Hurt, by Dennis & Matthew Linn and Sheila Fabricant (Mahwah, NJ: Paulist Press, 1985). Healing the deepest hurt most people experience, the loss of a loved one, through learning to give and receive love with the deceased in prayer through the Communion of Saints.

Purchase of Above Books & Tapes: Paulist Press, 997 Macarthur Blvd., Mahwah, NJ 07430 (201)825-7300

Videotapes on a Donation Basis: Videotapes for courses may be borrowed on a donation basis, in 1/2" VHS format, from: Christian Video Library, c/o Mary Ann Schmidt, 3914-A Michigan Ave., St. Louis, MO 63118 (314)865-0729.

Additional Audio Tapes: A wide variety of audio tapes by the authors on prayer, healing and related topics, including "Healing Our Image of God," is available from: ALU, 504 Antioch Lane, Ballwin, MO 63011 (314)227-7445.

Spanish Books & Tapes: Several of the above books and tapes are available in Spanish. For information contact ALU, 504 Antioch Lane, Ballwin, MO 63011 (314)227-7445.

Notes

PREFACE

1. *Psychology Today* (May, 1984), 44.
2. Marie Lawrence, OSF, "Psychosocial Development of Malcolm X through Erikson's Eight Stages," Thesis submitted to St. Louis University, December, 1974, 6.

INTRODUCTION

1. Toby Rice Drews, *Getting Them Sober II* (So. Plainfield, NJ: Bridge, 1983), 3.
2. Hugh Missildine, *Your Inner Child of the Past* (New York: Simon & Schuster, 1963).
3. Murray Bowen, *Family Therapy in Clinical Practice* (New York: Jason Aronson, 1978), 532.
4. Psychologists have documented how difficult it is to trust God if our sacred bond with our favored parent has been traumatically ruptured through death, divorce, or alcoholism. See Martin Lang, *Acquiring Our Image of God* (Mahwah, NJ: Paulist Press, 1983), 56. See also William G. Justice and Warren Lambert, "A Comparative Study of the Language People Use to Describe the Personalities of God and Their Earthly Parents," *The Journal of Pastoral Care*, 40:2 (June, 1986), 166–172. For a psychoanalytic study of the formation of our God-image and how it is affected by parents, see Ana-Maria Rizzuto, *The Birth of the Living God* (Chicago: Univ. of Chicago Press, 1979).
5. Steven Findlay, "Problems in Love & Marriage Lead Us to Therapists," *USA Today* (January 16, 1986), 4d.

6. Quoted by Dr. Thomas A. Harris, *I'm OK—You're OK* (New York: Avon, 1973), 2.

7. Erik H. Erikson, *Insight and Responsibility* (New York: W. W. Norton, 1964), 175.

8. Marie Lawrence, OSF, *op. cit.*

9. For a discussion of how emotional deprivation can be healed by parental substitutes, see Conrad W. Baars, M.D. and Anna Terruwe, M.D., *Healing the Unaffirmed* (New York: Alba House, 1976) and Conrad W. Baars, M.D., "When the Power to Heal Becomes Destructive," *Journal of Christian Healing*, 5:1 (Spring, 1983), 3–9.

10. For an account of how all these factors were involved in Linda's experience, see Dennis & Matthew Linn, S.J. and Sheila Fabricant, *Praying with Another for Healing* (New York: Paulist Press, 1984), Chapters 3 & 8.

11. See Nancy C. Andreasen, M.D., Ph.D., *The Broken Brain: The Biological Revolution in Psychiatry* (New York: Harper & Row, 1984), for a discussion of current research into the biochemical bases for mental illness.

12. Dag Hammarskjold, *Markings* (New York: Alfred A. Knopf, 1969), 89.

CHAPTER 1:
INFANCY (TRUST VS. MISTRUST)

1. Ashley Montagu, *Touching: The Human Significance of the Skin* (New York: Harper & Row, 1978), 78–79. See also Rene Spitz, "Anaclitic Depression," in *The Psychoanalytic Study of the Child*, 2 (New York: International Universities Press, 1946), 313–342.

2. "Colombian Doctors' Unique Concept Gives High-Risk Infants 95% Chance of Survival," *Houston Campaign for Child Survival* (newsletter of U.S. Committee for UNICEF, 1360 Post Oak Blvd., Ste. 225, Houston, TX 77056), 1:4 (Spring, 1987), pp. 1–3. Further information can be obtained from Marina Jaramillo, Fundacion Vivir, Carrera 20, #86A-42, Apartamento 403, Bogota,

Colombia, and from Hammersmith Hospital in London (where the "kangaroo method" is being tried).

A less radical method of treating premature babies with touch involved massaging them three times per day for fifteen minutes. After ten days, these babies had gained 47% more weight, performed better on the Brazelton scale and thus were released six days ahead of the non-massaged babies. Robert Trotter, "The Play is the Thing," *Psychology Today* (January, 1987), 34.

3. Arthur Janov, *The Feeling Child* (New York: Simon & Schuster, 1973), 120; James Prescott, "Body Pleasure and the Origins of Violence," *The Futurist*, 9:2 (April, 1975), 73–74. (While we appreciate Dr. Prescott's insight that touch is inversely related to violence, we do not share all his conclusions regarding the role of religion or moral values, e.g., his advocacy of pre- and extramarital sexual relationships. It seems to us that the deeper human need is intimacy—rather than touch—and that touch is one important way of meeting this need. Further it seems to us that touch can be used in nongenital ways which fulfill the need for intimacy, in situations where sexual expression is restrained for the sake of other values.)

Not only the brain but also the respiratory system may be affected by insufficient touch and bonding with the mother. An interesting example is a method of treating asthmatic children whose mothers were unable to bond with them at birth. Using hypnotherapy, the cause in the mother for the non-bonding was determined and treated. Then she was encouraged to regress to the pregnancy and birth and experience a new, bonded birth. At this point, in the cases reported, the child's asthma symptoms disappeared. Antonio Madrid and M. Xavier McPhee, "The Treatment of Pediatric Asthma through Maternal-Infant Bonding in Hypnosis," *PPANA Journal* (1985), 4–6.

4. Jack Panksepp, "Substitute Bonds—Drugs as 'Family,' " *Brain/Mind Bulletin*, 5:12 (May 5, 1980), 3; Prescott, *op. cit.*, 69 & 71.

5. Prescott, *op. cit.*, 64–74. See also a beautiful article by Robert Coles, comparing the attitudes of North American caucasians toward touch, with attitudes in other cultures: Robert

Coles, "Touching and Being Touched," *The Dial* (Public Broadcasting Corp. publication, December, 1980), 26–30.

6. Virginia Satir, reported in *Sojourners*, March, 1981.

7. Rebelsky & Hanks, "Fathers' Verbal Interaction with Infants in the First Three Months of Life," *Child Development*, 42 (1972), 63–68. As the infants studied grew older, 70% of their fathers decreased their verbal interaction time.

8. R. J. Trotter, "Fathers & Daughters: The Broken Bond," *Psychology Today* (March, 1985), 10.

9. Marshall Hamilton, *Father's Influence on Children* (Chicago: Nelson-Hall, 1977), 51.

10. *Psychology Today* (January, 1983), 71.

11. Frank Lake, *Tight Corners in Pastoral Counseling* (London: Darton, Longman & Todd, 1981), 14–37; R. Gaddini, "Early States and Neonatal Psychology," in L. Carenza & L. Zichella (eds.), *Emotion and Reproduction* (London: Academic Press, 1979), 1076–78; David B. Cheek, "Maladjustment Patterns Apparently Related to Imprinting at Birth," *Am. J. Clinical Hypnosis*, 18:2, October, 1975, 75–82.

12. David K. Spelt, "The Conditioning of the Human Fetus in Utero," *J. Experimental Psychology*, 38:3 (June, 1948), 338–46. Anthony DeCasper found that $7^{1}/_{2}$-month fetuses could distinguish between a story which their mothers had read to them many times before and an unfamiliar story, cf. *Psychology Today* (May, 1987), 4. Some have carried the idea of fetal memory to the extent of founding fetal education programs, cf., William Poole, "The First Nine Months of School," *Hippocrates* (July/August, 1987), 68–73.

13. Karl Pribram's theory of prenatal memory is that memory depends on protein molecules in the single cell rather than on complex neural connections. Frank Lake, *op. cit.*, 2 & 36.

14. Lyall Watson's theory is that memory is stored in a spiritual body that accompanies our spiritual body. Quoted in Morton Kelsey, *Afterlife: The Other Side of Dying* (New York: Paulist, 1979), 106–107.

15. Linda Mathison, "Birth Memories: Does Your Child Remember?," *Mothering* (Fall, 1981), 103–107.

16. Andrew Feldmar, "The Embryology of Consciousness: What Is a Normal Pregnancy?," in David Mall & Walter Watts (Eds.), *The Psychological Aspects of Abortion; Chicago Tribune*, "Embryos Can Remember, Therapist Says" (November 1, 1978). Support for Dr. Feldmar's work comes from others who have found a significant correlation between birth trauma and adolescent suicide. Cf., Lee Salk, et al., "Relationship of Maternal and Perinatal Conditions to Eventual Adolescent Suicide," *The Lancet*, I:8429 (March 16, 1985), 624–627. Dr. Bertil Jacobson also found that the suicide method tends to reproduce the specific type of birth trauma. E.g., people who committed suicide by violent means were more likely to experience mechanical birth trauma, such as forceps delivery; people who experienced asphyxia (loss of oxygen) at birth were more likely to commit suicide by asphyxia (e.g., hanging or gas poisoning). *The Denver Post*, "Trauma at Birth Associated with High Suicide Rates in Young Adults" (July 11, 1987), 10A.

17. Antonio J. Ferreira, "Emotional Factors in the Prenatal Environment," *J. Nervous & Mental Disease*, 141:1 (1965), 112–113; Ashley Montagu, *Life Before Birth* (New York: Signet, 1965), 156–71.

18. Thomas Verny, *Secret Life of the Unborn Child* (New York: Summit, 1981), 76.

19. D. H. Stott, "Follow-Up Study from Birth of the Effects of Pre-Natal Stresses," *Develop. Med. Child. Neurol.*, 15 (1973), 770–787.

20. Verny, *op. cit.*, 48.

21. Charles Spezzano, "Prenatal Psychology: Pregnant with Questions," *Psychology Today* (May, 1981), 49–57.

22. Verny, *op. cit.*, 22–23.

23. Clifford Olds, "Fetal Response to Music," *PPPANA News*, 1 (April, 1984), 2.

24. S. N. Bauer, "Science of Touch and Feeling Has Great Import for Preborn," *St. Cloud Visitor*, 71:24 (November 11, 1982), 1 & 11. See also Conrad W. Baars, M.D., *Feeling & Healing Your Emotions* (Plainfield, NJ: Bridge, 1979), 81–84.

25. Jerome Kagan, *The Nature of the Child* (New York: Basic Books, 1984), 109.

26. A recent study of mothers of 62 babies who failed to grow normally in the womb confirms Jennifer's experience. In these 62 cases no somatic cause (maternal or fetal) could be found for the intra-uterine growth retardation. After interviewing the mothers, researchers concluded that they were ambivalent during the pregnancy about their future child, and this manifested itself as a failure to "let it grow." In the best cases, such ambivalence can produce a hypotrophic child, but in more severe cases it could even mean prematurity, death in utero, etc. Researchers also noted the "frequent coincidence between a lack of maternal affection during a woman's childhood and the birth of a hypotrophic child in her adulthood." A. Raoul Duval, "Psychogenetic Aspects of Intra-Uterine Growth Retardation," *PPANA Journal*, 1:1 (1985), 10–13.

27. Ashley Montagu, 1978, *op. cit.* See also Rene Spitz, *The First Year of Life* (New York: International Universities Press, 1965). For a discussion of the diagnosis and treatment of severe emotional deprivation or "deprivation neurosis," see Conrad Baars & Anna Terruwe, *Healing the Unaffirmed: Recognizing Deprivation Neurosis* (New York: Alba House, 1976).

28. Meyer Friedman & Ray Rosenman, *Type A Behavior and Your Heart* (Greenwich, CT: Fawcett, 1974).

29. Redford B. Williams, Jr., John C. Barefoot & Richard B. Shekelle, "The Health Consequences of Hostility," to appear in M. A. Chesney, S. E. Goldston & Rosenman, R. H. (Eds.), *Anger, Hostility and Behavioral Medicine* (New York: Hemisphere/McGraw Hill, 1984). Quote is from p. 2 of unpublished manuscript.

30. *Ibid.*, 14–15.

31. There are many possible causes for homosexuality and lesbianism. According to Dr. Elizabeth Moberly, homosexuality and lesbianism are generally rooted in a failure to establish a bond of basic trust with the same-sex parent. Such a bond would allow the child to identify adequately with that parent as it develops. A failure of same-sex bonding and identification means that, as an adult, the homosexual or lesbian is still searching for

same-sex love and identification, and unable to enter the more unknown world of heterosexual relationships. Dr. Moberly's method of treatment is to heal early hurts with the same-sex parent and in therapy to provide the missed parental same-sex love (without genital expression). This allows the homosexual or lesbian adult to forgive the same-sex parent, make up for early emotional deprivation, establish a foundation of basic trust with the same sex, and then naturally develop into a capacity for heterosexuality. Elizabeth Moberly, *Homosexuality: A New Christian Ethic* (Greenwood, SC: Attic Press, 1983). See also Conrad W. Baars, *The Homosexual's Search for Happiness* (Chicago: Franciscan Herald Press, 1976).

32. R. Scott Sullender, *Grief and Growth* (New York: Paulist, 1985), 197.

33. Child-rearing authority Selma Fraiberg writes of children deprived of the love and touch which build basic trust as "likely to become bondless, hollow men and women who contribute largely to the criminal population. . . . Their nonattachment leaves a void in that area of personality where conscience can be. Where there are no human attachments there can be no conscience. The potential for violence is far greater among these bondless men and women. We must look upon a baby deprived of human partners as a baby in deadly peril. This is a baby who is being robbed of his humanity." In Selma Fraiberg, *Every Child's Birthright* (New York: Basic Books, 1977), 62.

34. Erik Erikson, *Childhood and Society* (New York: W. W. Norton, 1963), 251.

35. For a discussion of the use of sexual imagery for God, see Sandra Schneiders, *Women and the Word* (Mahwah, NJ: Paulist Press, 1986):

"No matter how entrenched in the imagination of the average Christian the image of a male God might be, theological tradition has never assigned sex to God. St. Gregory of Nazianzus well represented the tradition when he affirmed that the terms 'Father' and 'Son' as applied to the persons of the Trinity were not names of natures or essences but of relations and even in this case the terms are used metaphorically. In other words,

God is neither a father nor a son but the first person of the Trinity is related to the second person as origin is related to that which is originated. Because the ancients believed that God was indeed personal, and because their defective biology ascribed all agency in procreation or personal originating activity to the male partner, their choice of 'father' for the originating person of the Trinity was logical enough. And since they wished to affirm the absolute likeness and equality of the one originated to the divine principle they called the second person the 'son.' They were, however, quite aware of the metaphorical nature of their language and never intended to impute actual sexuality to the God whom Scripture affirms is pure Spirit (cf. Jn. 4:24)." (pp. 2–3)

Regarding Jesus' use of words like "Abba" and "Father," Dr. Schneiders writes of Jesus' continual presentation of himself as " 'the sent one,' " as "a son who is gradually initiated into his father's trade, apprenticed to his father until such time as he is able to take over the 'family business,' " i.e., to save the world. "This pervasive parabolic presentation of the integration of Jesus' work into the great salvific plan of God demanded that God be presented as father, that is, as the male rather than the female parent. In the patriarchal culture of Jesus a mother-son relationship could not have carried this meaning because mothers had no independent trades and they did not train their male children for adult work. The cultural constraints under which the mystery of redemptive incarnation took place demanded that Jesus experience himself as son of a divine father in order to describe the unique revelation of which he was the subject . . .

"The question, in other words, is not so much *why* Jesus experienced God as father. Jesus certainly did not experience God or think of God as exclusively masculine or he could not have presented God in feminine metaphors." (pp. 42–44)

Jesus' use of "Abba" was not meant to reveal the masculinity of God, but rather the intimate love of God: " . . . by his use of 'Abba' for God and his presentation of God as the father of the prodigal, Jesus was able to transform totally the patriarchal God-image." (p. 48)

In his article "Non-Patriarchal Salvation," Bernard

Cooke similarly argues that "Abba" is intended to reveal a non-patriarchal God, rather than a male one. In Joann Wolski Conn, (ed.), *Women's Spirituality* (Mahwah, NJ: Paulist Press, 1986), 274–286.

For a discussion of sexual imagery for the three persons of the Trinity, see also Elizabeth Johnson, C.S.J., "The Incomprehensibility of God and the Image of God Male and Female," in Conn, *op. cit.*, 243–260 (originally published in *Theological Studies*, 45 (1984), 441–465). "The critique brought by women theologians against the exclusive centrality of the male image and idea of God is not only that in stereotyping and then banning female reality as suitable reference points for God, androcentric thought has denigrated the human dignity of women. The critique also bears directly on the religious significance and ultimate truth of androcentric thought about God. The charge quite simply is that of idolatry. Normative conceptualization of God in analogy with male reality alone is the equivalent of the graven image, a finite representation being taken for and worshiped as the whole." (p. 245)

Johnson argues that each of the three persons of the Trinity is as much feminine as masculine, i.e., the first person is as much Mother as Father. Others, such as Donald Gelpi, propose seeing the first person of the Trinity as Father and the Spirit as the feminine, motherly side of God. Cf., *The Divine Mother: A Trinitarian Theology of the Holy Spirit* (Lantom: University Press of America, 1984). Johnson and others find this solution unsatisfactory, since it still assigns primacy or "first person" status to a male image. Moreover, since the Spirit is the most "faceless" of the three persons of the Trinity, we continue to believe that God and the capacity to originate life are primarily male. Arguing along these lines, if we're going to use the parent-child analogy to describe relationships within the Trinity, then we need to accept the implications of that analogy: i.e., if Jesus had a divine Father then he also had a divine Mother.

Theologians such as Schneiders and Johnson believe that Jesus used masculine words such as "Abba" and "Father" for cultural reasons and that such usage need not be considered normative today. Thus, today Jesus would call God "Mother" as well as "Father," and this would shock his listeners no more than "Abba" did 2000 years ago. Others, such as Gelpi, do consider gender references in Scripture as normative when speaking of individual persons of the Trinity. Whichever of these positions one takes on the individual persons of the Trinity, Johnson, Schneiders, Gelpi and many other Catholic scholars agree that when speaking of God in general one may use feminine as well as masculine images, as does Scripture.

36. Schneiders, *op. cit.*, 38–39.

37. The complete text of Pope John Paul I's 9/10/78 talk may be found under the title "Praying for Peace" in Matthew O'Connell (ed.), *The Pope Speaks*, (Huntington, IN: Sunday Visitor), 23:4, 314. See also "God Is Father and Mother," an English summary of Hans Dietschy's commentary in German on the Pope's words, in *Theology Digest*, 30 (1982), 132–33.

38. Pope John Paul II, "Rich in Mercy," footnote #52.

39. Theodore Irwin, "First Child? Second Child? Middle Child? Last Child? What's the Difference?," *Today's Health* (October, 1969), 26–27, 79–80, 84; Walter Toman, "Birth Order Rules All," *Psychology Today* (December, 1970), 45–46, 68–69.

40. Joanna Rogers Macy, *Despair and Personal Power in the Nuclear Age* (Philadelphia: New Society Publishers, 1983), 48–59.

CHAPTER 2:
EARLY CHILDHOOD (AUTONOMY VS. SHAME AND DOUBT)

1. Stanley & Nancy Greenspan have researched four stages in the development of autonomy. See Colleen Cordes, "Team Maps Children's Emotional Milestones," *Am. Psych. Assn. Monitor* (March, 1985), 32–33; Stanley & Nancy Greenspan, *First Feelings* (New York: Viking Press, 1985). By its second year the child knows the difference between right and wrong. It can begin to have empathy because it can move out of itself, and it knows it is wrong to hit another child. Cf. Jerome Kagan, *The Na-*

ture of the Child (New York: Basic Books, 1984), 126–27. For a summary of Kagan's book, see "What Shapes the Child?," *Newsweek* (Oct. 1, 1984), 95. See also John Bales, "Research Traces Altruism in Toddlers," *Am. Psych. Assn. Monitor* (January, 1984), 20–22.

2. Contrary to the impression given by Erikson and others of increasing separation from mother (and others) during the transition from infancy to the stage of autonomy, Daniel Stern writes, "The period of life from roughly nine to eighteen months is not primarily devoted to the developmental tasks of independence or autonomy or individuation—that is, of getting away and free from the primary caregiver. It is equally devoted to the seeking and creating of intersubjective union with another, which becomes possible at this age. This process involves learning that one's subjective life—the contents of one's mind and the qualities of one's feelings—can be shared with another. So while separation may proceed in some domains of self-experience, new forms of being with another are proceeding at the same time in other domains of self-experience." In Daniel N. Stern, *The Interpersonal World of the Infant* (New York: Basic Books, 1985), 10.

3. Cordes, *op. cit.*, 32.

4. *Ibid.*, 33. For a beautiful study of the suffering of the child who is not encouraged to experience the full range of its own emotions, see Alice Miller *The Drama of the Gifted Child* (New York: Basic Books, 1981).

5. Miller *op. cit.*, viii.

6. Arlene Skolnick, "The Myth of the Vulnerable Child," *Psychology Today* (February, 1978), 33.

7. Kenneth Pelletier, *Holistic Medicine* (New York: Delacorte, 1980), 11.

8. "The Hardy Heart," *Psychology Today* (January, 1987), 22.

9. Robert Karasek, *Prevention* (December, 1984), 75.

10. Sharon Wegscheider, *Choice-Making* (Pompano Beach, FL: Health Communications, 1985).

11. Kenneth Bailey, *Poet and Peasant* (Grand Rapids: Eerdmans, 1976), 164.

12. Louis Puhl (ed.), *Spiritual Exercises of St. Ignatius* (Westminster, MD: Newman Press, 1959), 141–50.

CHAPTER 3:
PLAY AGE (INITIATIVE VS. GUILT)

1. Erik Erikson, "Identity and the Life Cycle," *Psychological Issues*, 1:1 (1959), 74–76.

2. For a discussion of the inability of fear and guilt to create a loving person, see Paul Tournier, *Guilt & Grace* (New York: Harper & Row, 1983), Chapter 22.

3. See Alice Miller, *op. cit.*, Chapter 3, "The Vicious Circle of Contempt."

4. Erikson, *op. cit.*, 80.

5. Parents may unconsciously direct their unmet sexual needs at a child. These needs may also be expressed overtly, in the form of incest. Before the Oedipal theory, Freud originally suggested the "seduction theory," according to which cases of female hysteria were rooted in real experiences of sexual abuse in the patient's childhood, usually by her father. But because of cultural and personal factors, Freud and his colleagues eventually changed to the Oedipal theory, in which reports of childhood sexual victimization were regarded as wishful childhood fantasies. In other words, he shifted the blame from the parent to the child. Those who believe that sexual abuse occurs commonly and who challenge Freud's shift in theory insist "that when Freud arrived at the seduction theory, he did so by listening carefully and intently to his female patients; when he arrived at his Oedipal theory, he did so by listening carefully and intently to himself." Florence Rush, *The Best Kept Secret: Sexual Abuse of Children* (New York: McGraw-Hill, 1980), 95; Roland Summit, M.D., "Background, Identification and Evaluation of Child Sexual Abuse, *Childhelp USA Monograph Series*, 4 (June, 1983), 34. See also Miller, *op. cit.*, pp. 74–76 for a discussion of how narcissistic parents may unconsciously seduce their children.

6. Harold Kushner, *When All You've Ever Wanted Isn't Enough* (New York: Summit Books, 1986), 82.

7. Dennis Guernsey & Diane Bunker, "The Use of Representational Systems in the Healing of Memories," *Journal of Christian Healing*, 3:1 (Summer, 1981), pages 3–18. See also follow-up discussion, *Journal of Christian Healing*, 4:1 (Winter, 1982), 17–20.

CHAPTER 4:
SCHOOL AGE (INDUSTRY VS. INFERIORITY)

1. This study by Robert Rosenthal (Harvard psychologist) and Lenore Jacobson (San Francisco principal) is cited often, most recently in Alan Loy McGinnis, "Bringing Out the Best in People," *Reader's Digest* (October, 1986), 97–100.

2. See Alfie Kohn, "It's Hard to Get Left Out of a Pair," *Psychology Today* (October, 1987), 53–57. See also Alfie Kohn, *No Contest: The Case Against Competition* (Boston: Houghton Mifflin, 1986).

3. Mary Rowe, Ph.D., "Pausing Phenomena: Influence on Quality of Instruction," *J. Psycholinguistic Research*, 3 (1974), 203–224.

4. Friedman & Rosenman, *op. cit.*

5. Dag Hammarskjold, *Markings* (New York: Knopf, 1974), 122.

6. As Thomas Green points out, we are spiritually purifed not primarily by the dark night of the soul but by experiencing how much God loves us when we face failure and limitation. Cf. *Darkness in the Marketplace* (Notre Dame: Ave Maria, 1981). For others, purification may mean risking enjoyment of the success God wants to give them beyond what they believe they deserve.

7. Shirlee Monty, *May's Boy* (New York: Thomas Nelson, 1981).

CHAPTER 5:
ADOLESCENCE (IDENTITY VS. IDENTITY CONFUSION)

1. Erik Erikson, "Identity and the Life Cycle," *op. cit.*, 93.

2. *Ibid.*, 92.

3. Martin Lang, *op. cit.*, 61, 100–101.

4. Erik Erikson, "Once More the Inner Space," in *Life History and the Historical Moment* (New York: W. W. Norton, 1975), 243.

5. Erikson, "Identity and the Life Cycle," *op. cit.*, 93.

6. *Ibid.*, 92.

7. James Pennebaker studied the relationship between confiding in others and physical illness as an aftereffect of trauma. He found that sexual abuse is the traumatic event least likely to be confided in others, and that those who do not confide in another about an experience of sexual abuse are more likely to experience stress-related illnesses than those who do confide. James W. Pennebaker, "Traumatic Experience and Psychosomatic Disease: Exploring the Roles of Behavioral Inhibition, Obsession, and Confiding," *Canadian Psychology*, 26:2 (1985), 82–95; James W. Pennebaker and Claudia W. Hoover, "Inhibition and Cognition: Toward an Understanding of Trauma and Disease," in R. J. Davidson, G. E. Schwartz and D. Shapiro (Eds.) *Consciousness and Self-Regulation, Vol. III* (New York: Plenum Press, 1983).

8. Study by Diane E. H. Russell and published by the American Psychiatric Association. Reported in *Omaha World Herald* (September 20, 1984), 37.

9. Roland Summit, "Background, Identification and Evaluation of Child Sexual Abuse," *Childhelp USA Monograph*, 4 (June, 1983), 6.

10. Reported by Ruth Norton, New Lifestyles Program (treatment program for prostitutes), St. Louis, Missouri, 1985.

11. Terry Selby M.S.W., "Agonizing Aftermath of Abortion." Address given at Minnesota Citizens Concerned for Life 1984 State Convention.

12. *Psychology Today* (May, 1984), 44. However, not all

abused children repeat the cycle of abuse as adults. For a review of factors that stop this cycle, see Joan Kaufman & Edward Zigler, "Do Abused Children Become Abusive Parents?," *American J. of Orthopsychiatry,* 57:2 (April, 1987), 186–192.

13. Other sexual abuse victims may hide behind obesity. One study of sexually abused women found them to be an average of 28 lbs. overweight. Reported at the 1987 convention of the American Orthopsychiatric Association in Washington, D.C. This and other helpful information on diagnosis and treatment of sexual abuse is available on Tape #OR101.

14. Roland Summit, *op. cit.* and "Treatment of the Sexually Abused Child," *Childhelp USA Monograph,* 5 (June, 1983). Both these monographs are helpful resources for understanding the traumatic effects of sexual abuse. Available from: Childhelp USA, Research Division, 14700 Manzanita Park Rd., P.O. Box 247, Beaumont, CA 92223. The traumatic emotional effects of sexual abuse can even include growth retardation, or "psychosocial dwarfism," according to Dr. John Money, as reported in "Child Abuse Still Difficult to Detect," *Brain/Mind Bulletin,* 5:12 (May 5, 1980), 3.

15. *The Journal of Christian Healing* publishes articles on the integration of professional medical and psychotherapeutic practice with healing prayer. The Spring, 1984 (6:1) issue of the *Journal* focuses especially on healing sexual hurts. Address: 103 Dudley Ave., Narberth, PA 19072. For issues of emotional involvement with therapy clients vs. "clinical distance," see Baars & Terruwe, *Healing the Unaffirmed, op. cit.*

16. While the power of healing prayer is mediated by healthy human beings, it can also be blocked by unhealthy ones. Persons praying with sexual abuse victims whose own sexuality is insufficiently healed are in danger of projecting their own hurts and/or abandoning the person prayed for in the midst of the healing process, with disastrous consequences. See Conrad W. Baars, "When the Power to Heal Becomes Destructive," *Journal of Christian Healing,* 5:1 (Spring, 1983), 3–9. For more on praying with a sexually abused person, see Dennis & Matthew Linn and Sheila Fabricant, *Praying with Another for Healing* (New York:

Paulist Press, 1984), Chapters 3 and 8, and Talk #3 of the video-tape series *Praying with Another for Healing,* "Blocks to Healing Prayer," (see Appendix C).

17. For friendship as the basis of sexual relationships, see Mary Joyce, *How Can a Man and Woman Be Friends?* (Collegeville: Liturgical Press, 1977) and interview with Robert & Mary Joyce by Sheila Fabricant, "Understanding Our Sexuality," *Journal of Christian Healing,* 6:1 (Spring, 1984), 6–13.

18. For a beautiful study of the feminine as an overlooked aspect of reality, see Paul Tournier, *The Gift of Feeling* (Atlanta: John Knox Press, 1981).

19. Nancy Chodorow, *The Reproduction of Mothering* (Berkeley: Univ. of California Press, 1978). See also James B. Nelson, "Male Sexuality and Masculine Spirituality," *SIECUS Report,* 13:4 (March, 1985), 2.

20. Erik Erikson, *Identity: Youth and Crisis* (New York: W. W. Norton, 1968), 268–71.

21. Carol Gilligan, *In a Different Voice* (Cambridge, MA: Harvard University Press, 1982). See also Jean Baker Miller, *Toward a New Psychology of Women* (Boston: Beacon Press, 1976).

22. Evelyn Fox Keller, *Reflections on Gender and Science* (New Haven: Yale University Press, 1985), 158–176. A similar example is given from the field of primate research, where male scientists have emphasized the role of the dominant male in a primate community, while women scientists have recently noticed more cooperative social structures.

23. Gilligan, *op. cit.,* 15.

24. Joann Wolski Conn suggests we need " . . . a corrective to all present developmental frameworks that are biased toward autonomy. The latter consistently define growth in terms of differentiation and increasing autonomy, and lose sight of the fact that adaptation is equally about integration and attachment. As sensitive women and men are recently pointing out, the result of this bias has been that differentiation (the stereotypically male overemphasis in this human ambivalence) is favored with the language of growth and development, while attachment (the stereotypically female overemphasis) gets referred to in terms of

dependency and immaturity . . . if women are more vulnerable to fusion . . . it is also possible that they are more capable of intimacy . . . And if men find it easier to reach psychological autonomy—not to be confused with human maturity, it is also possible that they find it harder to evolve to more mature mutuality and relational inter-dependence . . . " Joan Wolski Conn, "Spirituality and Personal Maturity," in Robert J. Wicks, et al. (eds.), *Clinical Handbook of Pastoral Counseling* (New York: Paulist Press, 1985), 37–57. See also Robert Kegan, *The Evolving Self* (Cambridge, MA: Harvard University Press, 1982).

25. Ann Belford Ulanov, *Receiving Woman* (Philadelphia: Westminster Press, 1981), 134. Based upon an essay by Valerie Saiving Goldstein, "The Human Situation: A Feminine Viewpoint," in Simon Doniger (Ed.), *The Nature of Man in Theological and Psychological Perspective* (New York: Harper & Row, 1962), 151, 153, 165.

26. Erikson, *Identity: Youth & Crisis, op. cit.*, 293–94. In "Male Sexuality and Masculine Spirituality," *op. cit.*, James Nelson writes from his Protestant tradition that for men God is "experienced more as transcendent than immanent, more beyond than within. Such, characteristically, has been the shape of a male-dominated theology. The Protestant Reformation itself was strongly masculinist in mood and, among other things, it was a reaction against Roman church practices which had become 'too feminine'—too immanent, immediate, physical and sensual. Thus the Reformers attacked physical representations of the divine—relics, crucifixes, stained glass, images of the Virgin. The radical 'otherness' of God was recaptured, while the radical immanence of God faded. But this concept also applies to the spirituality of males generally. Orientation to mystery is more one of penetrating otherness than of embracing it within." (p. 2)

27. Joan Wolski Conn, "Restriction and Reconstruction," in *Women's Spirituality, op. cit.*, 14–16. See also Ana-Maria Rizzuto, *Birth of the Living God, op. cit.*, 180–202.

28. Quixote Center, *Set My People Free* (April, 1986), 11.

29. On the need to use inclusive language for God, Sandra Schneiders writes, "Important as correct ideas about God may

be, it is the imagination which governs our experience of God because it is the imagination which creates our God-image and our self-image. Consequently, if the demonic influence of patriarchy on the religious imagination is to be exorcised, if the neurotic repression of the feminine dimension of divinity is to be overcome, the imagination must be healed. It is absolutely imperative that language, which appeals to the imagination through metaphor, symbol, gesture, and music, be purified of patriarchal overtones, male exclusive references to God, and the presentation of male religious experience as normative. We must learn to speak to and about God in the feminine; we must learn to image God in female metaphors; we must learn to present the religious experience of women as autonomously valid." *Women and the Word, op. cit.*, 70–71. See also Elizabeth Johnson, *op. cit.* and Elisabeth Moltman-Wendel, *A Land Flowing with Milk and Honey* (New York: Crossroad, 1987).

30. Peggy Reeves Sanday, "The Socio-Cultural Context of Rape: A Cross-Cultural Study," *The J. of Social Issues*, 37:4 (1981). See also Ginny Soley, "Our Lives at Stage," *Sojourners* (November, 1984), 13–15.

31. Andrew Greeley, *The Religious Imagination* (New York: William H. Sadlier, 1981). Cited in Len Sperry, "The Male's Image of Self, Father and God: Development, Distortion and Healing," to appear in Sheila Fabricant (Ed.), *Sexuality and Healing* (Narbeth, PA: Journal of Christian Healing).

32. Ulanov, *Receiving Woman, op. cit.*, 170. We find in Ulanov's words a corrective to the viewpoint that God must be Father (and not Mother) because God is transcendent. An illustration of this viewpoint is Walter Ong, *Fighting for Life* (Ithaca: Cornell University Press, 1981), 174–177. While Ong's book contains excellent insights into male/female differences, it seems to us that his very emphasis on God's transcendence is an example of why we need to know God equally as Mother. When God is only Father, as for Ong, the transcendence of God is emphasized at the expense of God's immanence.

33. John W. Greene, et al., "Stressful Life Events and Somatic Complaints in Adolescents," *Pediatrics*, 75:1 (January,

1985), 19–22.

34. *Vital Statistics of the U.S. 1980, Vol. II,* "Mortality, Part A" (Hyattsville, MD: U.S. Dept. of Health & Human Services, 1985), 32.

35. George Valliant, *Adaptation to Life* (Boston: Little, Brown, 1977).

36. Carol Howard, "Teenagers at Risk," *Psychology Today* (November, 1985), 22–23.

CHAPTER 6:
YOUNG ADULTHOOD (INTIMACY VS. ISOLATION)

1. Paul Simon, "I Am a Rock."

2. Recently David McClelland discovered that Harvard undergraduates had more immunoglobin A secreted in their saliva to fight colds after watching a film of Mother Teresa intimately loving the destitute and dying. Even just watching an intimate person makes us healthier! Joan Z. Borysenko, "Healing Motives: An Interview with David McClelland," *Journal of Christian Healing,* 8:2 (Fall, 1986), 22–23.

3. Catherine Houck, "Psychosomatic Illness: More Than We Imagine," *Reader's Digest* (February, 1984), 141. A University of South Carolina study of Type A heart attack-prone persons found those with a social support network had healthier hearts with reduced narrowing of coronary arteries. *Psychology Today* (September, 1986), 10.

4. K. J. Helsing, "Factors Associated with Mortality After Widowhood," *Am. J. Public Health,* 71 (1981), 802–809. See also a study by James W. Pennebaker and Robin C. O'Heeron of spouses of suicide and accidental death victims which found that those who shared their feelings with friends had less illness following the death. "Confiding in Others and Illness Rate Among Spouses of Suicide and Accidental-Death Victims," *J. of Abnormal Psychology,* 93:4 (1984), 473–476.

5. Kenneth Pelletier, *Holistic Medicine* (New York: Delacorte, 1980), 93.

6. Elisabeth Kubler-Ross, *Death: The Final Stage of Growth* (Englewood Cliffs: Prentice-Hall, 1975), 160.

7. Intimacy is also a basic issue in chemical dependency. Many in Alcoholics Anonymous are discovering they are "clean as a whistle but miserable as hell." Earnie Larsen writes that intimacy is the key to a full and happy recovery. "From a recovery standpoint, both chemical dependency and co-dependency have to do with *intimacy* far more than they have to do with alcoholics or alcohol. He finds that recovering alcoholics have a terrible time believing they deserve anything good, especially an intimate relationship. Earnie Larsen, *Stage II Recovery: Life Beyond Addiction* (New York: Harper & Row, 1985), 16.

8. Jean Macfarlane, "Perspectives on Personality Consistency and Change from the Guidance Study," *Vita Humana*, 7:2 (1964). Reported in Arlene Skolnick, "The Myth of the Vulnerable Child," *Psychology Today* (February, 1978).

9. Daniel Levinson, *The Seasons of a Man's Life* (New York: Alfred A. Knopf, 1978), 335.

10. Julian Meltzoff & Melvin Kornreich, *Research in Psychotherapy* (New York: Atherton Press, 1970), 203, 331, 334.

11. This distinction between effectivity and affectivity, and its relationship to affirmation, is based upon an unpublished transcript of a talk by Dr. Anna A. Terruwe, "Affective Relationships in the Religious Community."

12. Conrad W. Baars, M.D., *Born Only Once* (Chicago: Franciscan Herald Press, 1975).

13. Conrad W. Baars, M.D. & Anna A. Terruwe, M.D., *Healing the Unaffirmed: Recognizing Deprivation Neurosis* (New York: Alba House, 1976), 4. In his article "When the Power to Heal Becomes Destructive," *Journal of Christian Healing*, 5:1 (Spring, 1983), 3–9, Dr. Baars discusses the role of affirmation in prayer for inner healing. See also a study of the importance of intimate love in psychotherapy by Dr. Elizabeth R. Moberly, *The Psychology of Self and Other* (New York: Tavistock Publications, 1985).

14. This section is based upon Conrad Baars, *Born Only Once*, op. cit., 23.

15. H. Norman Wright, *Communication and Conflict Resolution in Marriage* (Elgin, IL: David C. Cooke, 1977), 6.

16. Erik Erikson, *The Life Cycle Completed* (New York: W. W. Norton, 1982), 70.

17. For more on how the mature Christian lives out relationships of intimacy, generativity and integrity, cf. Evelyn & James Whitehead, *Christian Life Patterns* (Garden City, NY: Doubleday, 1979).

18. Jeanette & Robert Lauer, "Marriages Made to Last," *Psychology Today* (June, 1985), 22.

19. *Ibid.*, 22–26.

20. *Ibid.*, 26.

21. *Ibid.*, 25.

22. *Ibid.*, 24.

23. For a description of the Otts' couple prayer, see "Two Become One and Three" in Betty & Art Winter, *Stories of Prayer* (Kansas City: Sheed & Ward, 1985), 49–63.

24. Members of Adult Children of Alcoholics (ACOA) describe themselves as follows: "we became people pleasers . . . we preferred to be concerned with others rather than ourselves . . . we were terrified of abandonment . . . we learned to stuff our feelings down as children and keep them buried as adults . . . we confused love and pity, tending to love those we could rescue." But having learned compassion for themselves, ACOA members conclude, "This is a description, not an indictment." From "The Problem," ACOA/CSB, September 22, 1984.

25. Documents #72, 76, 801, 858, and 1306 in Denzinger-Schonmetzer, *Enchiridion Symbolorum, Definitionum et Declarationum* (Freiburg i. B.: Herder, 1963).

26. Richard McBrien, *Catholicism* (Study Edition) (Minneapolis: Winston, 1981), 1152. See also Karl Rahner (Ed.) *Sacramentum Mundi, I* (New York: Herder & Herder, 1968), 52, "Apocatastasis." For a scriptural study of the doctrine of hell, see William J. Dalton, *Salvation and Damnation* (Theology Today Series, #41; Butler, WI: Clergy Book Service, 1977), especially pp. 69–73 and 83. Dalton argues that while an eternal hell is an *abstract* possibility, given what we know of the loving nature of

God we may have real hope that all will be saved. For a more extensive discussion of our own view of hell, including the nature of purgatory, see Matthew & Dennis Linn and Sheila Fabricant, *Healing the Greatest Hurt* (Mahwah, NJ: Paulist Press, 1985), Chapter 5 and Appendix A.

CHAPTER 7:
ADULTHOOD (GENERATIVITY VS. STAGNATION)

1. Erik Erikson, *Gandhi's Truth* (New York: W. W. Norton, 1969).
2. "Gandhi," Columbia Pictures, 1982.
3. Harold Kushner, *op. cit.*, 172.
4. Major studies of adult growth and development include: Roger L. Gould, *Transformations: Growth and Change in Adult Life* (New York: Simon & Schuster, 1978); Daniel Levinson, et al., *The Seasons of a Man's Life* (New York: Ballantine, 1978); Gail Sheehy, *Passages: Predictable Crises of Adult Life* (New York: Dutton, 1976); George Valliant, *Adaptation to Life* (Boston: Little, Brown, 1977).
5. Carol Gilligan, *In a Different Voice* (Cambridge, MA: Harvard University Press, 1982), 74ff. See also Anita Spencer, *Seasons: Women's Search for Self through Life's Stages* (New York: Paulist Press, 1982), and report of study of Mills College students in Anne Rosenfeld & Elizabeth Stark, "The Prime of Our Lives," *Psychology Today* (May, 1987), 71.
6. Claude Steiner, *Scripts People Live* (New York: Grove, 1974).
7. Jean Vanier, *Community and Growth: Our Pilgrimage Together* (New York: Paulist Press, 1979).
8. M. Scott Peck, *A Different Drum* (New York: Simon & Schuster, 1987), 86–106.
9. Erikson's stages have an order. But as Joe discovered, they also occur together throughout life, with progress in one (e.g., generativity and reaching out) strengthening the others (e.g., autonomy and identity). Because stages of growth strengthen one another, A.A. suggests that an alcoholic like Joe

not wait for total healing before reaching out to another (A.A.'s twelfth and final step). Rather, Joe and other recovered alcoholics need to have enough development in the first eleven steps to be strong enough not to drink with the person they are helping, but not so strong as to think they don't need A.A. For both A.A. and Erikson, healing deepens as we reach out to give others the care we have received. One reason A.A. is so effective is that it respects growth as a process similar to the process of growth in Erikson's eight developmental stages. Although the program of A.A. does not refer to Erikson's stages, each of the eight stages are included in the twelve-step treatment program offered by A.A.

10. Constance De La Warr, *Mirror of Perfection* (London: Everyman's Library, 1973), 215.

11. Jean Vanier, *Man and Woman He Made Them* (Mahwah, NJ: Paulist Press, 1985), 23.

12. For more on the spirituality of mid-life, see L. Patrick Carroll & Katherine Marie Dyckmann, *Chaos or Creation* (Mahwah, NJ: Paulist Press, 1986).

CHAPTER 8:
OLD AGE (INTEGRITY VS. DESPAIR)

1. Erik Erikson, *Identity and the Life Cycle, op. cit.*, 98.

2. *Idem.*

3. George Ritchie and Elizabeth Sherill, *Return From Tomorrow* (Old Tappan, NJ: Revell, 1981).

4. Erikson, *Identity and the Life Cycle, op. cit.*, 98.

5. John Nicholson, "Coping with the Seasons of Life," *World Press Review* (November, 1980).

6. Erik Erikson, *The Life Cycle Completed, op. cit.*, 63.

7. Harold Kushner, *op. cit.*, 59.

8. Sr. Mary Jane Linn, C.S.J. and Dennis & Matthew Linn, S. J., *Healing the Dying* (Mahwah, NJ: Paulist Press, 1979).

9. Erik Erikson, *Identity: Youth and Crisis, op. cit.*, 141.

10. *Dying to Live* videotape series by Bill & Jean Carr and

Dennis & Matthew Linn, S. J. is published by Paulist Press. See Appendix C for more information.

11. Kathleen Fischer, *Winter Grace* (Mahwah, NJ: Paulist Press, 1985), 37.

12. *New York Times* (Feb. 21, 1984), C-1.

13. Harold Kushner, *op. cit.*, 171.

14. Walter J. Burghardt, S. J., *Seasons That Laugh or Weep* (Mahwah, NJ: Paulist Press, 1983), 86.

15. The religious vows of poverty, chastity and obedience follow Jesus' path of loving and being loved by God in the most threatening situations. The Israelites feared being without land, children, and freedom. Thus in God's love covenants with Israel, they are promised land (Gen. 12:15, Jer. 31:17), children (2 Sam. 7:12, Gen. 12:16), and freedom from slavery (Ez. 34:27; 2 Sam. 7:11). God also knew the blessing of being without land, without children, and without freedom. Thus Jesus came to us with no place to lay his head so that he might belong to all nations (Mt. 8:20), no children that he might belong to every family (Jn. 17:21), and a slave's existence that he might love by laying down his life (Phil. 2:7, Rom. 5:7). What God declares by treating Israel one way and Jesus in yet another is that any moment can be life-giving. The beatitudes also proclaim that the most threatening situations can lead us closer to God for nothing can separate us from God's love (Mt. 5:1–12, Rom. 8:31).

16. A Mass of generational healing is one of many ways we can pray for the deceased through the Communion of Saints. For a discussion of the psychological, theological and scriptural foundation for healing relationships with the deceased through prayer, see Dennis & Matthew Linn, S. J. and Sheila Fabricant, *Healing the Greatest Hurt* (Mahwah, NJ: Paulist Press, 1985).

APPENDIX A:
STUCK?

1. Elizabeth Kubler-Ross, *On Death and Dying* (New York: Macmillan, 1969)

About the Authors

FATHERS DENNIS AND MATTHEW LINN S.J. AND SHEILA FABRICANT, M.DIV. work together as a team, integrating physical, emotional and spiritual wholeness through their writings and retreats. They have taught courses on healing in many countries and universities, including a course for doctors that has been accredited by the American Medical Association. Their work has been translated and published in ten languages. All three are members of the Association of Christian Therapists and serve on the Board of Editors of the *Journal of Christian Healing*. Matt and Dennis are the authors of eight books, including *Healing of Memories, Healing Life's Hurts, Deliverance Prayer, Healing the Dying* (with Sr. Mary Jane Linn) and *To Heal as Jesus Healed* (with Barbara Shlemon). Together, Sheila, Dennis and Matt have written *Prayer Course for Healing Life's Hurts, Praying with Another for Healing,* and *Healing the Greatest Hurt* (all published by Paulist Press).